About the Authors

Daniel and Haley are 20-something Catholic converts who married young (eight years ago) and still really like each other. They'd like to think life looks like this:

But it usually looks more like this:

They've been blessed with three amazing kids under the age of five who bring joy and chaos to their lives. (Daniel and Haley haven't had a full night's sleep since 2009.) Daniel works full-time away from home and maintains their occasionally fruitful garden and always ornery flock of chickens. He enjoys running and knows way too much about *Star Wars*. Haley spends her days homeschooling their four-year-old, chasing babies, drinking coffee, and reading Jane Austen. She is also a free-lance writer and blogs at Carrots for Michaelmas.

Dedication

To four-year-old Benjamin who often expressed the great misery of having to wait five minutes for food to be photographed before digging in during the book-creating process. Your sacrifice is duly noted. We're so glad you entered our lives and motivated us to create traditions to pass on the Faith to you and your sisters. No praise is better than hearing you say we're the "best cookers." We love you.

And also to our wonderful parents who taught us that food and family go together and to Dr. Ralph Wood who introduced us to the beauty of the liturgical year.

Acknowledgements

Special thanks to Lauren Johnson for the family portraits, Margot Payne for making the most of her red pen, Daniel Hooker for his great cover design, and Garrett Payne for resizing all the photos when we didn't know how to.

Table of Contents

Introduction **8**

A Few Notes **11**

What Is the Liturgical Year? A Gift! **13**

Feasting with the Saints and Martyrs **16**

How Do I Get Started? **20**

November:

The Feast of St. Andrew, November 30 **(Tahini Tilapia)** **22**

The Season of Advent **25**

Practical Ways to Observe Advent **28**

Simple Advent Meals **(Simple Black Beans and Rice)** **32**

Advent Reflection: First Advent **34**

December:

The Feast of St. Nicholas, December 6, Simple Gifts **37**

Advent Reflection: The Darkness of Advent **39**

The Twelve Days of Christmas **42**

Christmastide, **(Christmas Stuffed Apples)** **44**

Christmas Reflection: The Incarnation and the Pietá **47**

January:

Epiphany, January, **(Three Kings Cocktail)** **49**

The Feast of St. Thomas Aquinas, January 28, **(Costarelle di Maiale alla Laziale)** **51**

February:

Candlemas, February 2, Celebrate with Candles **55**

Mardi Gras and Carnival, **(Sazerac)** **57**

March:

Simple Lenten Meals, **(Baked Tilapia with Cilantro Cream Sauce)** **60**

Observing Lent **63**

Lenten Reflection: Cleaning Up Our Souls **65**

Feast of St. Turibius of Mogrovejo, March 23, **(Lomo Saltado and Aiji Sauce)** **68**

April:

Eastertide, **(Nasturtium Salad)** **71**

Feast of St. George, April 23, **(Haley's Shepherd's Pie)** **74**

May:

Feast of the Mexican Martyrs, May 21, **(Rajas con Crema)** **78**

Feast of St. Michael Ho-Dinh-Hy, May 22 **(Vietnamese Peanut Sauce)** **81**

June:

Feast of St. Charles Lwanga, June 3, **(Ugali and African Chicken Stew)** **83**

July:

Feast of St Maria Goretti, July 6, **(Simplified Pasta Pescatore)** **87**

Feast of St. Augustine Zhao Rong, July 6, **(Fried Rice)** **90**

Feast of Sts. Anne and Joachim, July 26, **(Moules Marinières)** **93**

August:

Feast of St. Rose of Lima, August 23, **(Pancit Bihon)** **96**

Feast of St. Raymond Nonnatus, August 31, **(Catalan Picada Chicken)** 99

September:

Feast of Blessed Mother Teresa of Calcutta, September 5, **(Garden Fresh Curry)** 103

Feast of the Archangels, September 29, **(Roasted Michaelmas Chicken and Mashed Turnips)** 106

October:

Feast of St. Francis Borgia, October 10, **(Simple Spanish Tapas, Spanish Eggplant Spread, Potatoes Aioli)** 111

Feast of St. Ignatius of Antioch, October 17, **(Mujaddara, Hummus, and Cucumber and Yogurt Salad)** 116

November:

Martinmas (Feast of St. Martin of Tours), November 11, **(Stuffed Butternut Squash)** 120

We Begin Again **125**

Introduction

by Daniel

This book is the result of many hours in our garden, in our kitchen, and around our dining room table. We're not trained chefs or professional food photographers. We're just a young Catholic couple who want to learn how to observe the liturgical year and raise our children in the Faith. Our front yard is full of garden beds of veggies and squawking chickens, and our backyard is full of children digging in the dirt and playing hide-and-seek. We wouldn't have it any other way.

As Haley and I moved towards Catholicism, we also moved towards a more complete celebration of the Christian year. Starting with Michaelmas 2009, we tried to find traditional ways to celebrate the major feasts of the Church. **But it turned out to be far more difficult than we thought.** Part of the difficulty is that we do not live in a homogeneous

Christian culture with ancient traditions, a common food culture, or a close connection to the agricultural systems that sustain us.

When we began to look about for guidance on how to begin observing the liturgical seasons and feasts of the saints, most of the resources we found were kid-friendly crafts or recipes for cakes, cookies, and other desserts decorated to honor a certain saint. There's certainly a place for those things, but we wanted more.

For one thing, our kids are allergic to gluten and we try to avoid giving them excessive amounts of sugary food so a lot of those recipes were automatically out. But, deeper than that, **when observing the Christian Year we want to honor the ancient and global aspects of our faith while also celebrating the bounty of good food God gives us.**

In some ways, we're at a disadvantage when trying to celebrate the Church year. If you were a farmer in pre-modern England, celebrating Michaelmas (the Feast of the Archangels) on September 29th would come quite naturally. Blackberries would be ripe, the goose would be fat, apples and carrots would be ready to harvest while daisies lined the side of the road. You would know exactly how to prepare these things because your parents taught you and your neighbors were feasting in similar ways.

But we're not farmers in pre-modern England. We're probably the only ones in our neighborhood who celebrate this feast. We don't grow apples. Here in North Florida, blackberries ripen in May, not September. Carrots are a crop we can't even plant until fall for a winter growing season. And Haley has expressly forbidden me from killing any of the Canadian geese that roam our city.

So, we've done our best to adapt traditional recipes to our own little corner of the world. We often substitute ingredients here and there to suit what we happen to have in the garden (and you should feel free to do the same). We found many recipes and foods that are traditionally eaten on certain feasts. For other feasts, we couldn't find traditional meals so instead we prepared recipes from a saint's hometown or the place of their ministry.

We've learned a lot about saints, gardening, and cooking. Many of these feasts have become important family traditions. Skipping Michaelmas, for instance, is simply out of the question.

We hope this little book helps you begin celebrating:

1. The Christian year.
2. The lives of the Saints and Martyrs.
3. The global Church.
4. The earth's bounty.
5. The goodness of creation.

A Few Notes

Welcome to Our Table

These are the recipes and reflections that have grown out of our quest to learn about the liturgical seasons over the past four years. We grew food in our garden, prepared meals together, and took pictures of it in our dining room.

We're not great photographers, the presentation isn't perfect, and we don't know the first thing about photo editing. But welcome to our dining room with poor lighting, sticky floors, and remnants of LEGO creations on the table. Pull up a chair. We're glad you're here!

Notes on the Recipes and Real Food

We cook for a family of four (the baby isn't eating solids yet) so all the recipes should serve four and you will likely have some leftovers, too.

These recipes are inspired by a real food diet. Almost all are gluten-free or have gluten-free options. But we aren't extremists so not every ingredient is ideal. At our house we get farm fresh eggs from our chickens every day, but occasionally we fry things in vegetable oil instead of lard or a better "real food" option. So, we're not perfect, we're just trying. Feel free to adapt these recipes to what best suits your family!

For most of Christian history, eating healthy and ethically-produced food that doesn't harm the environment was a lot easier to do than it is now. Almost all food was "seasonal" and "organic" while most livestock was treated humanely, especially in comparison to modern factory farms. This is not meant to discredit all modern agriculture, grocery stores, and nutrition science. However, we have lost much in our divorce from the source of our food. The important point is that what we eat and how we treat creation is not incidental to our celebration of our faith.

We should ask ourselves, were the men and women who grew this food afforded dignity and a living wage? Were the animals given the care due to them as unique creatures of God? Was the land treated with harmful farming practices? It may not always be possible to grow or purchase the perfect ingredients for our meals, but we still must be aware of these questions.

Notes for Other Christian Traditions

While we observe the Christian Year to grow in our Catholic faith, the liturgical year can be celebrated by all Christians. You don't have to be Catholic to enter in to the liturgical seasons and learn about holy men and women of the Faith. In fact, it seems that in recent years, many Protestant Christians are rediscovering the rhythms of the Christian calendar and observing seasons like Advent and Lent. This is a wonderful and exciting way that the splintered Church can join together and celebrate our faith, despite theological differences.

What Is the Christian Year? A Gift

by Haley

"The liturgical year is not an idle discipline, not a sentimentalist definition of piety, not an historical anachronism. **It is Jesus with us, for us, and in us, as we strive to make His life our own.***"*
(Joan Chittister, *The Liturgical Year*)

The man who introduced me to the Christian Year isn't a Catholic; he's an East Texas-born Baptist, my favorite college professor, and a scholar of religion and literature. I clearly remember so many of his lectures, which he delivered in his big, booming voice. And I remember the painfully-truthful criticism that he wrote on the first paper I submitted for his class: *"Ms. Payne, unfortunately, no one has ever taught you how to write."* Ouch! Followed by one of the most generous gifts ever offered to me: *"Please allow me to have that honor."* When I left his class, I was a better writer and a better thinker, but I am particularly indebted to him for introducing me to the Christian Year.

He began a lecture for our Literary Classics of Christianity class, by drawing a line across the white board. He then drew two upward marks, evenly spaced. He labeled the first *"Easter"* and the second *"Christmas."* *"This, friends, is what most of us in the South have grown up believing are the events of the Christian year. Wait -- I've forgotten the Fourth of July,"* and he added a mark in the middle of the timeline.

Growing up in the South as an Evangelical Protestant, I knew he was right. Every Sunday at church feels pretty much the same, except for those three days. Easter we had lilies. Fourth of July we sang, "God Bless, America," and Christmas was the last Sunday that we had to hear someone belt out, "O, Night Divine" as a solo.

"But this isn't the whole story," he told us. He started to add marks to the timeline. And not just marks for individual holy days, but also for entire blocks of time. There weren't just a handful of special days to add; there

were *entire seasons* I had never known about! He started out at the beginning, which for the Christian Year isn't January 1, but *Advent*, the four weeks before Christmas.

In detail, he explained what the seasons were, why they existed, what they meant, how they prepared us for the season that followed, and how, as a whole, **they told us the story of Redemption**. He explained the darkness and the preparation of Advent, with its symbolic color of purple — the color of the bruised and penitent heart. The sorrow of the world waiting for a Savior, followed by the joy of the Incarnation. God loved the waiting world enough to become a helpless child, to be born as a human baby, homeless, and naked.

And Christmas isn't just one day! It's a season — 12 days of feasting, celebrating, and joy. And then the Season of Epiphany arrives: we remember the Wise Men, traveling from distant lands and how Our Lord didn't come for only one people group, but for all. We celebrate Him as the Light of the World.

Then, after these weeks of preparation, followed by celebration and feasting, we have "Ordinary Time," with its color of green. Time to live and work and pray — a season for *growing*.

Then comes Lent, as winter's chill prepares to give way for spring. Again, purple, for our hearts are in darkness. We fast, pray, and give, in order to clear our spiritual vision and to see ourselves as we truly are: in desperate need of God's grace. We seek to have true penitence for our sin. We ask God to transform us.

Good Friday arrives, its color black, its complete and utter darkness, when Our Savior dies for our guilt. And then, the brightness of Easter, after those long, cold, difficult 40 days of Lent. The great joy of a Risen Savior, after we stopped still, to mourn the Passion of Our Lord.

And there was more! Pentecost! Saints' days! Feasts and fasts and days to remember, observe, and celebrate! It was such a rich tapestry, telling the cosmic story, and I was hooked.

What a beautiful gift the Church offers us in the Christian Year! We get to wait for Christ, walk with Him, die with Him, and be raised with Him. We get to use food, music, and traditions, to help remind us what story we participate in: the cosmic tale of God's love. We get to live by a different calendar -- one that isn't created by greeting card and candy companies. A rich calendar of redemptive time that makes us take a breath, slow down, grow, change, remember, mourn, and sometimes really kick up our heels and party with joy. **It is the opportunity to set your life by a different watch, by holy time.**

Feasting with the Saints and Martyrs
by Daniel

People often describe the Church as "making" saints but this is inaccurate. **God makes saints, the Catholic Church merely recognizes them.**

Remembering the Saints

When I was still a Protestant living in New Orleans, it seemed that the Catholics of that city were always looking for any excuse to have a party. Every holiday had its own parade. Every birthday, football victory, and minor achievement was cause for an extravagant celebration. Since I had no concept of the Church Year at that point, my perception may not have been entirely accurate. But, now that I'm Catholic, I think I have a better idea of where they're coming from. Maybe those New Orleanians get a little carried away at times, but they're right that there are some things that require a healthy dose of celebration.

The saints are holy men and women who have become truly like Christ. They show us how to live, intercede for us, and cheer us on to glory as the great cloud of witnesses described in the book of Hebrews. What a great reason to have a feast!

The General Roman Calendar, which lists the different feast days throughout the year, actually only holds a fraction of the thousands of saints formally recognized by the Church. **Each day brings an opportunity to learn about amazing men and women of God who took seriously Christ's command to leave everything and follow him.**

Praising their Virtues

All Saints are similar in that they have become like Christ. Yet, they are all so different in the way they reflect the Glory of God for us. The calendar of saints is filled with warrior kings and pacifist monks, popes and farmers, rich benefactors and poor hermits, illiterate peasants and the most brilliant scholars who've ever lived. All saints are virtuous, but their virtue shows forth in a myriad of ways. In some, we see great courage, in others humility, in others profound charity. As we learn about the saint, we recognize these virtues and seek to imitate them in our own lives.

Praying with the Saints

One of the greatest misunderstandings between Christian traditions is the veneration of the saints, especially regarding prayer. As Catholic Christians we pray to the saints, but perhaps this practice is better described as praying *with* the saints or asking for their prayers. Just as we would ask a holy friend to pray for us, we ask the saints, our friends in heaven, for this same gift. Our relationship with these "friends of God" does not divert our attention from Jesus but instead directs our hearts to Him.

Celebrating the Church Universal

In this book, we've included saints from all over the world. This isn't a shallow attempt at a diversity quota but a true representation of the Universal Church. **Christ is victorious and he makes saints everywhere he sends his Gospel.** When we celebrate the feast of a saint from a place far away from us, we celebrate the global reality of our faith. We remember our brothers and sisters who are separated from us by geography, language, and culture and yet are united with us in Christ.

Petitioning for the Persecuted Church

Here in America, it can be easy to forget that persecution of Christians is common in many parts of the world. Christians are not only discriminated against legally but are arrested, beaten, and exiled. Their homes and churches are burned and holy sites are desecrated. **Many Christians are even killed for their faith, becoming martyrs for the name of Jesus.** We should pray whenever we can for our persecuted brothers and sisters, that God would give them strength and protection. We should also thank God for their profound faithfulness and powerful witness.

When we celebrate the feast of a saint who was martyred, we remember those who are still dying for their faith. Additionally, when we celebrate a saint from a place where Christians are now being persecuted, we pray specifically for those people.

Introducing Children to the Saints

Children learn through their senses and celebrating feast days through food and activity is a wonderful way to introduce children to the saints of the Faith. Here are some practical ideas for sharing the saints with children:

- Get children in the kitchen, helping to prepare the meal with you.

- Discuss how the meal reminds us of the saint or the region where he lived and served.

- Pull out maps and globes and learn about where the saint was born or where she ministered.

- Discuss the way Christians live in those areas today and pray for the persecuted Church.

- Read about the saint's life and note the great virtues he or she displayed.

- Discuss with your children how they can do little things to increase those virtues in your family to display God's love to those around you.

How Do I Get Started?
by Haley

A great place to begin observing the seasons of the Christian Calendar is the beginning of the Liturgical Year (Advent) in late November or early December, depending on the year. But, there's no reason you can't jump right in at the end of February, the middle of June, or any other time.

One of the things I hear from many families who are interested in observing holy time is that they feel overwhelmed because there are so many feasts. And it's true, there are multiple saints remembered each day of the year! But you don't (and can't!) observe everything.

A great way to begin is to just start celebrating saints' days that are significant to your family: name days, patron saints' days, etc. For example, we have a daughter named Lucy so it's likely that in December, we will celebrate St. Lucy's feast and another feast that has become a family tradition: St. Nicholas's Day. But we may not celebrate other wonderful feasts like Our Lady of Guadalupe or St. Juan Diego. There isn't time to do everything and one facet of observing holy time is to go by a different watch than our hurried, frantic culture does. The point is not to get stressed out by the Liturgical Year! It is a gift that offers us rhythm and space to breathe. Choosing two days a month to celebrate is a great beginning.

November 30: St Andrew

by Daniel

About the Saint

St. Andrew was a fisherman, brother of Simon Peter, friend and apostle of Christ, evangelist, and martyr. Andrew was first a disciple of John the Baptist and, according to John the Evangelist, was the first disciple called by Christ. After Christ's Death, Resurrection, and Ascension, St. Andrew went out to preach the Gospel. He travelled as far north as the Black Sea (which is why he is patron saint of Russia and the Ukraine) and was finally martyred in Achaea, Greece. Ancient sources say Andrew was bound, not nailed, to a cross. Iconography from the Middle Ages shows his cross raised in the shape of an X, hence the familiar "St. Andrew's Cross" on the Scottish flag.

Tahini Tilapia

This seafood dish is made in remembrance of St. Andrew's first profession. Although we don't know exactly what kind of fish St. Andrew ate, tilapia have been caught in the Sea of Galilee since ancient times. Although not named in Scripture, they've been known as "St. Peter's fish" and are thought to be the fish St. Peter pulled from the water, to find a coin in its mouth, in Matthew 17.

Ingredients

4 tilapia fillets

1 medium onion, thinly sliced

2 TBSP tahini

2 TBSP olive oil

1 lemon, halved

½ tsp paprika

½ tsp cumin

salt and pepper

1. If your tilapia fillets are frozen, be sure to let them defrost ahead of time. Preheat the oven to 400 degrees F. Oil a baking dish and lay the fish out. Squeeze ½ of the lemon over the fish and sprinkle with salt.

2. Combine the tahini, olive oil, juice from the other half of the lemon, paprika, cumin, and salt/pepper. Mix together to make a thick sauce.

3. Cover the fish with the tahini mixture and toss the onion slices on top. Drizzle a little extra olive oil over the onions and sprinkle with a pinch of salt.

4. Bake the fish in the oven for about 15 minutes. It should be white all the way through in the thickest part. I like the onions to get a little crispy, too. Serve with rice, couscous, quinoa, or flat bread and a simple seasonal vegetable.

Saint Andrew Christmas Novena

(Pray 15 times daily, from the Feast of St. Andrew to Christmas Day)

Hail and blessed be the hour and moment in which the Son of God was born of the most pure Virgin Mary, at midnight, in Bethlehem, in piercing cold. In that hour, vouchsafe, O my God! to hear my prayer and grant my desires, through the merits of Our Saviour Jesus Christ, and of His Blessed Mother. Amen.

The Season of Advent

by Haley

For most Americans, the days between Thanksgiving Day and Christmas Day are a time to be with family, to be thankful for all we have, and to give whatever we can to those in need. There's certainly nothing wrong with that! But it's not news that Christmas has been secularized. For Christians, this season should be about so much more than what our culture offers us. Every year, I hear Christians bemoaning the secularization of Christmas -- yet the solution seems so simple.

If we want Christmas to be a religious holiday for our families, the way to get beyond the red and green M&Ms and the hustle and bustle is to take the time to prepare ourselves spiritually. **To make Christmas mean something, we must observe the traditional season of Advent.**

The Church has such a beautiful rhythm of celebrating the various seasons of the Christian story. The four weeks before Christmas (a little after Thanksgiving until December 25th) is the season of Advent.

Advent (not New Year's) is the beginning of the Christian Year and it's considered a 'little Lent.' It's quiet. It's somber. It's full of waiting and hoping. Just as there can be no real celebration of the Resurrection without the pain of Good Friday, there can be no real Christmas without the expectation of Advent.

St. Charles Borromeo writes, "*Each year, as the Church recalls this mystery, she urges us to renew the memory of the great love God has shown us. This holy season teaches us that Christ's coming was not only for the benefit of his contemporaries; his power has still to be communicated to us all…The Church asks us to understand that Christ, who came once in the flesh, is prepared to come again. When we remove all obstacles to his presence he will come, at any hour and moment, to dwell spiritually in our hearts, bringing with him the riches of his grace.*"

Isn't that beautiful? But that kind of preparation doesn't just happen *to* us. We have a part to play. We have to offer this time to ready our hearts for Our Lord. If you really commit to observing Advent, your December is going to look very different.

For most American families, by the evening of December 25th, we have been eating, buying, Christmas music-listening, gift-giving, gift-receiving, tree-trimming, and cookie-baking for over a month. We're sick to death of it: *Get the tree out by the road! Take the decorations down the day after Christmas! Turn that blasted music off!*

If you observe Advent, before Christmas Day arrives you might not be tree-trimming and you might not be holiday-cheering. But, you will know every verse of "O Come, O Come Emmanuel" by heart and you'll be itching to belt out "Joy to the World!" on Christmas morning.

You'll be reflecting, reading, praying, and waiting. And it will be a sacrifice. What will it look like for your family? You might decide to forego all the Christmas parties that happen during Advent. You might avoid the malls, which blare Christmas music starting in October. You might decide to keep gifts super simple, so that you're not doing any scrambling during the quiet of Advent and can, instead, focus on waiting for Jesus. The practicalities of how you decide to observe Advent will vary from family to family. But if you do set aside this time as a holy preparation, it's a surefire thing that in comparison to the bustle around you, your family will look quite odd.

Before you label me as the modern Ebenezer Scrooge, let me tell you a secret: We don't delay the merry-making because we hate the Christmas season; we observe Advent because we *love* Christmas.

If we observe the quiet Advent Season of expectation, then on Christmas Day, it will feel like CHRISTMAS! And it lasts for *twelve* days. It's a Christmas-lover's dream come true! We've been waiting and waiting and waiting. We've been lighting candles and watching the wax melt a little lower each night. We've been setting up a Jesse Tree and remembering God's story of Redemption for the world and how the Incarnation is the point on which it all spins. The tree-trimming, the carol-singing, the feasting, the celebrating — there are twelve whole days of it! We wait and wait through the long days of Advent, like a pregnant woman in her last month. Then, when we celebrate the joyous Birth of Our Lord, it is time to kick up our heels! And we do. We really do.

As you contemplate what Advent will look like in your home, consider this inspiration from St. Charles Borromeo:

"Beloved, now is the acceptable time spoken of by the Spirit, the day of salvation, peace and reconciliation: the great season of Advent. This is the time eagerly awaited by the patriarchs and prophets, the time that holy Simeon rejoiced at last to see. This is the season that the Church has always celebrated with special solemnity. We too should always observe it with faith and love, offering praise and thanksgiving to the Father for the mercy and love he has shown us in this mystery."

Make your Advent Season one of focus: Ignore the rushing and the bustling. Prayerfully prepare yourself for Jesus' coming. Christmas Day is approaching. Have you made room in your heart for the Christ Child?

Practical Ways to Observe Advent

by Haley

It's overwhelming to envision what it looks like to redeem the Season of Advent because in popular culture these weeks have, unfortunately, morphed into a pre-Christmas season of holiday shopping. Here are a few ideas for observing Advent with your family plus some suggestions of events to avoid, in order to keep it a simple and quiet season. But keep in mind that just because these "dos and don'ts" help our family keep focus during Advent, it doesn't necessarily mean that they will be a perfect fit for *your* family. For instance, we avoid holiday parties until Advent is over, but maybe there's a special party that is a family tradition at your house. Maybe it makes Advent "feel" like Advent and helps you gain the expectation of Christmas Day. Great!

The big picture is pursuing things that help prepare *your* heart for the Christ Child -- however that looks for *your* family.

(And please don't sacrifice family relationships for a rigid set of Advent rules! The point is the intention of your heart -- not whether you successfully avoided "Santa Baby" until December 25th. If you always bake Christmas cookies with your grandma the first week of December, you should go ahead and bake those cookies and enjoy those special moments.)

Some Advent Suggestions

We sometimes refer to Advent as a "little Lent." Adding some Advent spiritual disciplines such as attending daily Mass, going to Adoration, spending time in prayer, and giving to a charity can help us open our hearts to Jesus. Here are some more ideas to help you ready yourself to celebrate the Incarnation on Christmas morning!

- **Eat simple meals.** Help distinguish between the feasting of Christmastide by keeping meals simple during Advent.

- **Bring out your Nativity Scene.** I have great memories of setting up the Nativity Scene in our living room when I was a little girl. It is a wonderful way to explain the Incarnation to young children and engage them in the story. You can either bring it out all at once or set out one piece each day and reserve "Baby Jesus" for Christmas Morning. Some families even set out the various pieces of the set in distant corners of the house and each day during Advent, they move the characters and animals a few inches toward the crèche (the little framework that houses the scene) as they "act out" the journey toward Bethlehem.

- **Do a Jesse Tree**. The Jesse Tree's ornaments tell the "big picture" story of Redemption. You add one ornament each day to a simple tree. Each ornament represents Old Testament stories of God's great story of love for humanity. The ornaments can be made out of circles of wood, felt, or paper. You can paint the wood, glue felt designs onto the felt, or color the circles of paper.

- **Light your Advent candles.** For us, the Advent wreath and candles are always a central part of the season and a beloved family tradition. We always order a beeswax Advent candle-making kit because it's so easy for children to roll the sheets of beeswax into candles. We read Scripture lessons as we light the candles and we sing "O Come, Divine Messiah," one of our favorite Advent hymns.

- **Decorate the house with simple greenery and save the rest for Christmas Day**. We just go to the Home Depot or Lowe's Christmas Tree sales area and ask to take home branches that they cut off of the Christmas trees. They've always sent us home with a trunk full of free greens!

- **To Tree or Not to Tree:** Some families wait until Christmas Eve to set up their Christmas Tree and some set it up just after Thanksgiving. I like the symbolism of waiting until Christmas Eve but I also love the wonderful tradition of driving to a Christmas Tree Farm outside of town with Daniel's whole family and cutting down a tree in mid-December. It's one of the kids' favorite days of the year.

(Remember what I said about not getting caught up in Advent "rules"?) We string lights on the tree but we don't decorate with ornaments until Christmas Eve. The lights remind us that we're waiting for the Light of the World.

●

- **Use an Advent Calendar.** We have an Advent calendar of little storybook ornaments. Each evening, we read one of the storybooks and then hang it on the tree. Our four-year-old, Benjamin, really loves reading these together and it's so hard for him to wait for the next day to read the next "chapter."

- **Find a "Messiah Sing-Along."** Some cities have the tradition of hosting a performance of Handel's beautiful masterpiece. In this community tradition, the audience sings. It's been my favorite Advent tradition ever since I was a little girl. You bring your score or rent one there; sit with your fellow altos, sopranos, tenors, or basses; and sing your heart out.

- **Listen to Advent music.** I keep a Spotify playlist of some of our favorite Advent songs. We also love the albums *Advent at Ephesus* and *In the Bleak Midwinter* by Marian Grace, featuring Colleen Nixon.

- **Take time to pray and read spiritual writings.** *Watch for the Light* has some wonderful and beautiful Advent selections by folks like Thomas Merton and Dorothy Day.

- **Give.** Charitable giving is one holiday tradition that is a perfect fit for Advent! Sacrificing our time or money for the needy helps us to remember the big picture. Have your children help you pick out a charity and save up as a family. Make peanut butter bird feeders for the birds. Give away clothes and toys to those who need them more than you do.

Traditions to Save for Christmas Day

- **Listening to Christmas music.** This is a tough one. It's torture for me to wait until Christmas to listen to my favorite Christmas songs but it's an Advent discipline that's worth the sacrifice. It's so exciting to play Christmas music all during Christmastide after weeks of anticipation. And feel free to sing "Frosty the Snowman" whenever you like . . . it's not actually about Christmas—it's about winter.

- **Going to Christmas parties.** We don't attend holiday parties, unless they are scheduled after Christmas Day. It helps us keep things simple and also keeps our schedule relaxed, so that Advent doesn't become stressful. We've started a tradition of having lots of friends over, sometime between Christmas Day and New Year's Eve, to sing Christmas carols and eat holiday snacks. So, if you're worried about missing out on holiday festivities, just create your own -- within the appropriate season.

- **Watching Christmas movies.** Yes, as with Christmas music, it's so hard to wait, but worth it!

- **Make Christmas cookies.** We have a set of Nativity cookie cutters and the little ones love it when it's time to bake and decorate.

Simple Advent Meals
by Haley

In the midst of Christmas music blaring everywhere you go and Christmas lights appearing in your neighbor's yard the first day of November, it's difficult to simplify your Advent and to remember that the party of Christmas hasn't started yet. One way we remind ourselves of this fact is by eating simple meals (mostly vegetarian) as an Advent discipline. It reminds us that we're still waiting and still hoping for Christ's coming.

Simple Black Beans and Rice

Because it's such an easy and frugal dish, we eat Black Beans and Rice often -- but especially during Advent and Lent. It's vegetarian and simple, without being bland, and the kids love it. These directions are for using a slow cooker, but you could cook the beans on a pot over the stove. We had great luck with bell peppers and banana peppers in our garden this year, so that's usually what we add, but feel free to use whatever vegetables are in season where you are!

Ingredients

2 cups black beans (dry)

5 cups water

2 TBSP olive oil

1 onion, diced

5 cloves garlic, minced

3 bell peppers, chopped

2 bay leaves

4 tsp cumin

6 tomatoes or 1 can (14.5 oz, undrained)

Salt and pepper – to taste

1. Add the dry black beans, water, and tomatoes to the slow cooker. Cook on low for 4-6 hours. Check beans to see if they are almost done (every slow cooker is different). When the beans are almost ready, add the other ingredients and cook for an additional hour.

2. Serve with rice or corn chips and garnish with sour cream and cilantro. We always add Sriracha sauce to ours for a little extra spice!

First Advent
by Haley

I was huge. Not just big — gigantic. Even before I entered my third trimester, well-intentioned old ladies would pat my shoulder encouragingly and say, "Any day now!" as I waddled my way through the grocery store. Considering the raging pregnancy hormones running through my system, I'm impressed that I didn't slap any of the kind-hearted dears. I was huge.

As the end of November neared, I started wearing flip-flops exclusively because my swollen feet wouldn't fit into anything else. I think I gave up on other footwear after one particularly bad day when my husband had to help me get my boots off as I helplessly yelled inchoate phrases about being the only woman who would be pregnant *forever*. My maternity coat didn't fit anymore by the time it was cold enough to wear it. When I wasn't at work, I was lying on the couch or in the bathtub, trying to remember what it felt like to be able to see my toes. But then I would see a tiny limb change position — reminding me that my massive tummy housed a moving, living child.

As December neared and Advent began, I considered this season for perhaps the first time. I had lighted Advent candles as a little girl, and had been excited about Christmas coming, but had never considered the season as anything except a Pre-Christmas countdown. I came to realize that this is as incomplete an understanding of Advent as a definition of pregnancy as merely the nine months preceding a birth.

While I tried to remember what my feet looked like, I remembered the Blessed Virgin Mary. I confess that I had never thought much about her before. I had never felt that we had anything in common until now. But as my belly got rounder and rounder and my back got achier and achier, I remembered her. *She has done this,* I thought. *She has felt her child move in her womb, perhaps responding to the sound of her voice or her song. She experienced this miracle of life, taking place within her.*

In our modern disenchanted age, we have not completely lost our fascination with the miracle of new life. Whenever I dragged my sleepy pregnant body to public places, my experience was different than ever before. Little children looked at my belly, fascinated, sometimes even trying to give my belly a pat or lift up my shirt to discover if there was really a baby inside. Other mothers smiled at me and grandmothers reassured me. My ordinary child, this new ordinary life, elicited such a response of amazement. I began to wonder, *How much more miraculous is the coming of our Lord?*

For unto us a child is born. Unto us a son is given.

I was expecting my son during the season of expectation. The word comes from *expectare*—to wait, to hope, to look for. I did all these things. At first, there was contentment in the waiting and in the hoping. But eventually, the groaning, miserable discomfort led to a readiness to be delivered and face labor. A week before my due date, I was so exhausted and so tired of bumping the counters with my colossal tummy and getting up 10 times a night because the little angel had given my bladder yet another energetic punch, that I began to lose it. I couldn't climb the stairs to my office one more day. I couldn't fit behind my desk. I couldn't sleep.

Until the discomfort crossed a certain threshold and I was struck with a desperate desire to be pregnant not a day longer, the pain of delivery was alarming to me and I remained unprepared. But in those last days, it no longer frightened me. *Anything but this.* **I started to understand that it is not until we are exhausted, ill with our condition, and miserable, that we are ready for Christ — only then can we really long to be delivered.**

I kept thinking about the Blessed Virgin Mary. *Was she as desperate to give birth as I was?* I considered with wonder how, when her baby boy was delivered, he would in turn deliver her, deliver me, and deliver my own unborn son.

As I waited in joyous, miserable, anxious expectation, I started to understand an inkling of what it must have felt like to wait for the Messiah, Mary's son. I begin to understand the Joy born to the world on Christmas Day and present with us now as I heard the sound of the first beautiful and strong cry of my newborn son. I realized, in a new way, how to wait with groaning and expectation for our Lord's return in glory. It was my first Advent.

December 6: St. Nicholas

by Haley

About the Saint

Until recently, I didn't know anything about St. Nicholas except that Santa Claus is his strange holiday descendant of sorts. What I found out surprised me: St. Nicholas was nothing like his jolly, rosy-cheeked, red-suited, cookie-snarfing counterpart, who is concerned with everyone's "niceness." He was a fighter for the truth — literally. From examinations of this holy bishop's relics in Bari, Italy, it's clear that he sported a seriously broken nose. It appears to be broken multiple times and some legends even claim he grew up as a street fighter. We know he was kicked out of the Council of Nicea for punching the infamous heretic, Arias, in the face. Arias taught the heresy that Christ was not fully divine and St. Nicholas couldn't listen to another word.

While I'm not advocating punching heretics in the face (and he did get in big trouble for his violence) I can't help but love St. Nicholas for his fiery passion for the truth.

This saint was also courageous and compassionate. Upon hearing that three innocent men were going to be executed, St. Nicholas ran to the scene and demanded that the executioner put down his sword. The courage and authority of the saint halted the execution and the prisoners were freed. (Or maybe the executioner heard about what happened to Arias.) When St. Nicholas heard that a poor man's three daughters had no money to marry and would likely be forced into prostitution, he anonymously provided them each with a generous dowry. This may be how the tradition of giving gifts to children on St. Nicholas Day got started.

Simple Gifts

At our house, we exchange gifts on St. Nicholas Day instead of Christmas Day. It's traditional to fill children's shoes with little presents so we buy each child a new pair of shoes, fill them with little edible treats, and wrap up any other little gifties we're giving our little ones. Presents at our house are a simple affair, but we don't want them to be the focus of Christmas Day -- so we enjoy them together on a different day. In general, our Advent Season is pretty somber: lots of vegetarian meals, simple soups, and quiet evenings. St. Nicholas Day is a bright spot!

St. Nicholas Prayer

Loving God, we thank you for the example of St Nicholas, who fed the hungry, brought hope to the imprisoned, gave comfort to the lost, and taught the truth to all. May we strive to imitate him, by putting you first in all we do. Give us the courage, love, and strength of St Nicholas, so that, like him, we may serve you, through loving our brothers and sisters. Amen.
-Amy Welborn (used with permission)

The Darkness of Advent

by Haley

"O Come, O Come, Emmanuel" has always been my favorite carol. I love the ancient chant-like melody and the images it evokes: monks singing by candlelight and waiting to celebrate the coming of the Light of the World, while a cold, dark winter lingers on. It has many beautiful verses but the first and most familiar is:

O Come, O Come, Emmanuel
And ransom captive Israel
That mourns in lonely exile here
Until the Son of God appear.
Rejoice! Rejoice!
Emmanuel shall come to thee, O Israel

It is, of course, a particularly fitting verse for Advent, when we prepare for the Coming of Our Lord. Two years ago, Advent was a particularly dark season when dear friends of ours lost a child at birth. Their incomprehensible grief and the loss we have all experienced, as we miss their daughter, who we will never have the opportunity to know, made the uncertainty of this life more present.

We are not guaranteed lives free of pain. In fact, quite the opposite is true. We wait in exile. And in exile, there is grief. So, I have struggled with the darkness of our exile. *How do we live in a world of grief, pain, and uncertainty? How do we love those around us, knowing that we might lose them? What does it mean to wait for Jesus?*

St. Bernard of Clairvaux writes of three Advents. One is in the *past*: Christ was born to the Blessed Virgin Mary, when God Incarnate came to rescue the world. One is in the *present*: now is the time to prepare our hearts for Christ's dwelling. And one is in the *future*: Christ will come again in glory.

During the Advent Season, I usually consider only the past Advent: Christ's Nativity. It is complete and all I need to do is remember what has happened and celebrate on Christmas morning what Our Lord has done. The other two Advents require much more from me. *How do I prepare my heart for the Son of God to enter? And perhaps even more difficult: How can I bear waiting for Christ's return while in exile amidst grief, pain, and uncertainty?*

The Advent carol tells us that the first step is to long for Christ. *O come, O come, Emmanuel,* God with us. We long for Him because we have come to understand the difficult reality of our situation. **Until we realize that placing our security in anything of this life is fruitless, we will not be able to long for Christ, as we ought.** We are captives in this exile and we must understand our helplessness and need of a Savior. I remember Zechariah, who was struck dumb during the miraculous pregnancy of his aging and previously barren wife, Elizabeth. Waiting. Yearning for new life, as he anticipated the birth of his son, John the Baptist.

And ransom captive Israel, that mourns in lonely exile here... Our exile. It seems very dark. But we have been given a gift: a promise that our exile will not last forever. **We have been given hope. And our hope is a Living Hope, for it is Christ himself.** What makes the darkness and the waiting and the pain bearable is that it will come to an end. Zechariah will speak at the end of nine months. A woman's labor pains will end.

Until the Son of God appear... In the darkness of our exile, we wait in joyful hope because **He is coming. He HAS come. And He IS here.** *Rejoice! Rejoice! Emmanuel shall come to thee, O Israel.* **The Redemption of the world has happened in the Incarnation, it is happening in us and in the world, and it will be fulfilled and completed.**

How can we bear our exile? I don't pretend to know the answer. But I think I am learning that the key is **hope.** With hope we can say with Lady Julian of Norwich, even through our grief . . . *"And all shall be well, and all shall be well, and all manner of thing shall be well."* Note that she doesn't say, "Everything's OK." Everything is not OK. She says *"All shall be well."* What a difference. All shall be well. Not because our will has been done, but because Our Lord walks beside us, in our suffering, and he has conquered death with the power of his Love.

This pain, this exile, is not the final word. At the moment when the Word became flesh, God Himself, born as a baby in a cold stable with only his Blessed Mother, St. Joseph, and the angels to celebrate his coming: that is the moment of triumph, upon which the whole universe spins. We can hold onto this truth during the darkness of Advent.

Light of the World, though you have never left us, come again. Have mercy and give us hope.

Hail, Holy Queen, mother of mercy:
Hail, our life, our sweetness, and our hope.
To thee do we cry, poor banished children of Eve;
to thee do we send up our sighs, mourning, and weeping in this valley of tears.
Turn then, most gracious advocate, thine eyes of mercy towards us;
and after this our exile show unto us the blessed fruit of thy womb, Jesus.
O clement, O loving, O sweet Virgin Mary.
Pray for us, O holy Mother of God.
That we may be made worthy of the promises of Christ.

The Twelve Days of Christmas

by Haley

About the Season

Contrary to what retailers might have you believe, the Twelve Days of Christmas are *not* the twelve days that *precede* Christmas. They actually begin on Christmas Day, lasting until the Feast of Epiphany on January 6th. This season, also known as Christmastide, is traditionally when the holiday celebrating *starts* (but you'd never know it from all the Christmas trees already stripped bare and left by the curb on December 26th). If you have been observing Advent, you're probably chomping at the bit to begin celebrating Christmas just like we are!

12 Ideas for Celebrating

1. Go to Mass!

2. Decorate your Christmas tree with family ornaments and popcorn/cranberry garlands.

3. Enjoy festive meals.

4. Watch your favorite Christmas movies.

5. Drive around town to see Christmas lights with hot cocoa in hand.

6. Make special Christmas cookies.

7. Have friends over to sing carols.

8. Make paper snowflakes.

9. Make Gingerbread houses.

10.   Find a Las Posadas celebration in your area.

11.   Make a Twelfth Night cake.

12.   Snuggle up with your family's favorite Christmas books.

Christmas Apples

by Haley

About the Season

After the simple meals of Advent, it's exciting to celebrate Christmas with some really special meals. This is a festive dessert to enjoy on one of the Twelve Days of Christmas!

Ingredients
(For the apples and filling:)

6 apples

¼ – ½ cup brown sugar or "sucanat"

½ cup butter (softened)

¾ cup raisins

½ cup dried dates

½ cup chopped almonds

3 tsp cinnamon

½ tsp nutmeg

1 tsp clove

(For the sauce)

½ cup sugar

½ cup heavy cream

¼ cup butter

4 TBSP rum

1. Preheat oven to 350 degrees F.

2. Create a well in each apple by coring part way. (You don't want to core all the way to the bottom of the apple or else the stuffing will fall out.)

3. Mix all the other ingredients together, to make the filling. Stuff the filling into the wells that you made in the apples.

4. Bake in the oven (with just a little water in the bottom of the dish) until the apples are tender (approximately 1 hour).

5. While the apples are baking, combine the sauce ingredients in a saucepan and barely bring to a boil. Reduce heat and simmer 5 minutes, stirring frequently. Remove from heat and add rum. Drizzle the sauce over the apples, when they come out of the oven.

Prayer for the Feast of the Nativity

Let the just rejoice, for their Justifier is born. Let the sick and infirm rejoice, for their Saviour is born. Let the captives rejoice, for their Redeemer is born. Let slaves rejoice, for their Master is born. Let free men rejoice, for their Liberator is born. Let All Christians rejoice, for Jesus Christ is born.

St. Augustine of Hippo (AD 354-440)

The Incarnation and the Pietá

by Haley

The Incarnation of Christ, celebrated in the liturgical season of Christmastide, takes on a richer significance for me with each passing year. The story of the Nativity is fuller -- but undeniably stranger. It loses the saccharine quality of greeting cards and becomes complicated. **Christmas becomes more intricately connected to Holy Week and I'm reminded that the miracle of the Incarnation isn't merely that Our Lord was born as a human on the very earth I walk on, but that He came in order that He might die.**

The wooden manger foreshadows the wooden Cross, where His life will be extinguished. The joyful songs of angels, at Our Lord's birth, precede the agony of the heavenly hosts at his Death. The wise men bring myrrh -- perfumed ointments for funeral preparations -- to point to Our Lord's true purpose in visiting this planet. The ecstasy the Blessed Virgin must have experienced, when she first beheld Him, brings to mind her unrivaled suffering, as she watched His torturous Passion. **It is all one. It is all connected—God's unfathomable love and sacrifice for humanity.**

In some artistic renderings of the Nativity scene (I have Giuseppe Vermiglio's *Nativity and Adoration of the Shepherds* in mind), there is a strange image included in the stable. It is a lamb, but not a cuddly creature watching and adoring the precious Baby Jesus. It is a lamb with its legs bound, the sacrificial lamb that will be taken to slaughter. It reminds us, as St. John the Baptist does, that **when we see the Christ Child, we are beholding the Lamb of God, Who will carry our sins to the Cross.**

I had a strange experience at the Christmas Mass this year. We sang this beautiful hymn:

What child is this, who, laid to rest,
On Mary's lap is sleeping?
Whom angels greet with anthems sweet,
While shepherds watch are keeping?
This, this is Christ the King,
Whom shepherds guard and angels sing:
Haste, haste to bring him laud,
The babe, the son of Mary.

In the past, this song has always evoked an idyllic image of the Infant Christ, contentedly snoozing in His Mother's arms. But when I heard the words this year, I did not think of Bethlehem; instead, I saw Golgotha. I saw a grieving Mother Mary cradling the dead body of Our Lord. I saw the *Pietà*, Michelangelo's masterpiece that cries out in its sorrow and beauty, *Behold, God's love for you.*

The Nativity isn't cute. It isn't clean. The God of the Universe is born among animal dung, right in the thick of humanity's filth. He comes to give up everything, including His very life. **But it is an undeniably beautiful scene because it is an image of God's unwavering love.** His coming is the moment that all creation has waited for, with tears and groaning, like a woman in labor. Everything hinges upon it.

Perhaps if we did not suffer, we could see the Nativity as merely heart-warming and leave it at that. But in this our exile, we grasp at the truth of the Incarnation. We cling to the Cross, where our Savior's arms are outstretched, and He cries out, *"Behold, God's love for you."* **And this most grotesque and most beautiful of all images, the Crucifixion, is what makes the Incarnation our source of hope.** The true King has come to offer Himself as a sacrifice for us: To heal what is broken and to set all things right. His sacrifice, His death, becomes His triumph and our salvation. *Take heart, I have overcome the world.* And knowing that, we can sing "Joy to the World" with full hearts.

January 6: Epiphany

by Daniel

About Epiphany

The twelfth day after Christmas Day is the Feast of the Epiphany. Observed on January 6th, this feast celebrates the three kings' visit to the Christ Child and the revelation that Jesus is the Saviour of the whole world. It's become a family tradition on this day to read T. S. Eliot's "The Journey of the Magi."

The Three Kings Cocktail

The pomegranate is often seen in Christian art as a symbol of Christ's Passion and Resurrection and is a traditional food that Greek Christians eat during the Christmas season.

Ingredients

2 TBSP Gin

tonic water

lime

pomegranate seeds

1) Fill a glass with ice and a handful of pomegranate seeds.

2) Pour in two tablespoons of gin, fill the rest of the glass with tonic water, add a slice of lime, and mix together. If you crush some of the pomegranate seeds, the drink will turn red.

January 28: St. Thomas Aquinas
by Daniel

About the Saint

St. Thomas Aquinas holds a special place in our hearts because his writings, which we encountered in college, helped bring us to the Church. St. Thomas was a 13th century Dominican priest and scholar from Aquino, Italy, who made gigantic contributions to theology, philosophy, and Academia. For these reasons, he was made a Doctor of the Church, which was a recognition of his importance and of the trustworthiness of his teachings. Even secular scholars consider him to be one of the most important Western thinkers. It would be difficult to overstate his genius and holiness.

Toward the end of Thomas' life, Christ visited him while he was celebrating Mass. As a reward for all of his work, Christ offered to give him whatever he desired. When asked what he wanted, Thomas replied, "*Only you Lord. Only you.*" After this, Thomas experienced an ecstasy and saw a vision. He never told anyone what he saw but he no longer desired to write. When a friend suggested that he take up his pen and finish his books, Thomas replied, "*I cannot, because all that I have written seems like straw to me.*" That's probably worth thinking about.

Costarelle di Maiale alla Laziale

This recipe of grilled pork chops is made in the Lazio style since St. Thomas was from Aquino which is in the Lazio region of Italy. We serve this entrée with garlic herb butter and grilled sweet peppers.

St. Thomas Aquinas said many brilliant things. Among them was, "*Sorrow can be alleviated by good sleep, a bath, and a glass of wine.*" So, enjoy this with a bottle of Sangiovese or Chianti, two wines from the Lazio region.

Ingredients

4 thickly-cut pork chops

red wine

olive oil

italian bread, thickly-sliced

salt and pepper

1 head of garlic

1 stick of butter

1 handful of fresh sage, chopped

1) Lay the pork chops out in a glass casserole dish and splash them with wine and olive oil: use just enough liquid to coat the meat and to leave a little sitting in the bottom of the dish. Generously sprinkle the chops with salt and pepper. Flip the chops a few times so that they have an even coating of this quick marinade. Let the pork chops sit for about an hour.

2) Cut the top off the garlic head and wrap it in aluminum foil. Start grilling the garlic while the meat marinates. Cook the whole head until it's soft -- about 20 minutes or so.

3) Peel three of the garlic cloves and mash them into the butter. Add the sage along with salt and pepper. Mix thoroughly. Peel the other garlic cloves and refrigerate: the sweet flavor will be great in other recipes.

4) Thickly-cut pork chops are difficult to grill because you need to sear them first and then finish grilling them with a slow heat. The best way to do this, on a charcoal grill, is to pile the coals on one side so that you have one hot section and one cool section. Sear the chops quickly on the hot section -- about one minute. Then flip the chops and sear the other side. Move them to the cooler section of the grill. Continue grilling, until the internal temperature of the chops is 135 degrees F. Remove the chops from heat and let them rest for 10 minutes. During this rest, the meat will continue to cook in the center until it's about 145 degrees F.

5) While the meat rests, drizzle olive oil over the bread and grill each side until crispy. Serve the pork chops with the sage butter, crispy bread, and a simple side, such as grilled vegetables. And red wine, of course.

St. Thomas Aquinas Prayer for Guidance

O creator past all telling, you have appointed from the treasures of your wisdom the hierarchies of angels, disposing them in wondrous order above the bright heavens, and have so beautifully set out all parts of the universe.

You we call the true fount of wisdom and the noble origin of all things.
Be pleased to shed on the darkness of mind in which I was born,
the twofold beam of your light and warmth to dispel my ignorance and sin.

You make eloquent the tongues of children.
Then instruct my speech and touch my lips with graciousness.
Make me keen to understand, quick to learn, able to remember;
make me delicate to interpret and ready to speak.
Guide my going in and going forward, lead home my going forth.
You are true God and true man, and live for ever and ever. Amen.

-St. Thomas Aquinas

February 2: Candlemas
(The Presentation of Our Lord)

by Haley

About the Feast

This feast celebrates the Presentation of Christ: the event described in the Gospel of Luke, when the Virgin Mary and St. Joseph present Jesus at the Temple. Faithful Simeon and Anna behold and recognize Jesus as the Messiah, for whom they have been waiting. This feast, which occurs forty days after Christmas, is also in honor of the Purification of the Blessed Virgin Mary.

Celebrate with Candles

It is traditional, on this day, for the priest to bless candles intended for use in observing the Christian Year. Many parishes have a blessing ceremony for candles during Mass on Candlemas. So, if you are able, go to

Mass, present your Advent candles and any other religious candles that you intend to use during the Church Year, and have them blessed by the priest. And, if you're crafty, you can make your own candles from beeswax.

Beeswax

Before the use of paraffin became common, candles were made from beeswax. It has always been the traditional choice for liturgical candles (which are still at least 51% beeswax). But beeswax is used for other reasons: it burns pure without leaving a smoky residue, it has a lovely scent, and it's symbolic. When our daughter, Lucy, was baptized and received a candle (representing the light of Christ) our priest explained that the bee is a symbol of Christ Himself, Who tirelessly labors for his Church.

"The bee is more honored than other animals, not because it labors, but because it labors for others"
(St. John Chrysostom, 12th Homily).

There are plenty of reasons to avoid the toxic ingredients that many candles contain. Also, stocking up on beeswax candles for liturgical purposes is a great opportunity to seek out beeswax from local apiaries (bee farms) and to support your local bee farmer!

You can also order beeswax online, to make your own candles. Each year, we love ordering our Advent candle-making kit from Toadily Handmade Beeswax Candles and the kids really enjoy the process of making them!

Prayer

(When he finally beholds the Infant Christ, Simeon prays the *Nunc Dimittis* in Luke 2:29-32):

Lord, you now have set your servant free,
to go in peace as you have promised;
For these eyes of mine have seen the Savior,
Whom you have prepared for all the world to see,
A Light to enlighten the nations, and the glory of your people Israel.

Mardi Gras falls 47 days before Easter Sunday which is a moveable feast.

Mardi Gras and Carnival
by Daniel

About the Season

In the past, Lenten fasts, beginning in February or March, depending on the date of Easter Sunday, were much more demanding, forbidding not only meat but all animal products. In some places, the devout would also abstain from alcohol. To dispose of all this excess, people often consumed meat and alcohol at huge celebrations before the beginning of Lent on Ash Wednesday. The last day of this unofficial "Carnival" season is Fat Tuesday: Mardi Gras.

Some of these celebrations have become quite excessive -- even bizarre. Drunken debauchery is, of course, never a good way to celebrate anything. But parades, parties, and feasts are all fine ways to share in a culture and enjoy ourselves, especially if the revelry gives way to a season of introspection and repentance. There are thousands of Carnival foods and drinks from all over the world but I chose a simple cocktail from New Orleans, where I grew up.

Sazerac

Consumed in New Orleans since well before the Civil War, the Sazerac is now the official cocktail of the Big Easy. Bitters and absinthe make this drink unique and, although they may not be standard ingredients in every liquor cabinet, small bottles of each are inexpensive and will go a long way.

Ingredients

rye whiskey

bitters

absinthe

sugar cube (or simple syrup)

lemon peel garnish

1. Beforehand, chill one glass in the freezer. In a second glass, add three dashes of bitters, one sugar cube (or 1 teaspoon of sugar), and two ounces of rye whiskey. Muddle together, until the sugar has dissolved. Drop in a few ice cubes and stir (don't shake!).

2. Pour a splash of absinthe into the chilled glass and swirl around, to coat the sides. (This is mostly for the strong aroma of the absinthe, so you don't need much.) Strain the whiskey mixture into the absinthe-coated glass.

3. Rub the lemon peel around the rim of the glass and serve.

Simple Lenten Meals

by Haley

About the Season

As important as it is to celebrate joyous feasts, like Christmas and Easter, it's equally important to prepare our hearts during Advent and Lent. Lent lasts for 40 days but it always seems longer. This is the season in which we stop and remove distractions so that we can truly see ourselves and how much we need God's mercy. Take the time to embrace silence, listen to God, and examine your heart -- so that when Easter arrives, you are prepared to dance with joy and celebrate the Resurrection.

About Lenten Disciplines

Maybe you'll plan to give up entertainment, such as streaming Netflix, and replace that time with devotional reading or prayer. Maybe you'll give up that hot cup of coffee in the morning, as a tiny reminder of how much Jesus sacrificed for you. Lenten disciplines vary from person to person but we take them up to lead us closer to the Cross. For many of us, disciplines involving our meals are effective. Because food-related disciplines require us to literally control our physical appetite as a form of spiritual renewal, they are a healthy practice for tempering all of our appetites and ordering them toward loving God.

Meatless Meals

Catholics abstain from eating meat (in this case, the meat from fowl or mammals) on Fridays, as a sign of penance because Our Lord was crucified on a Friday. During most of the year, the Church recommends meatless Fridays as a penance but you may choose an alternate penance. In the season of Lent, however, Catholics age 14 and older are under obligation to forego meat on Fridays, barring special circumstances, such as pregnancy, sickness, etc.

Baked Tilapia with Spicy Cilantro Cream Sauce

My inspiration for creating this recipe for Baked Tilapia with Spicy Cilantro Cream Sauce came from the years we lived in Texas: There was a Mexican seafood restaurant in Waco that served an amazing Stuffed Tilapia dish. When I was pregnant with our son, Benjamin, I craved this dish at least once a week, and I decided to try to recreate it.

Ingredients

4 fillets of tilapia

olive oil

1 pint heavy whipping cream

1-2 cloves of garlic, minced

1-2 TBSP lime juice

one handful of cilantro, chopped

1/3 cup to 1/2 cup grated Parmigiano Reggiano

Seasonings (to taste):

Black pepper, salt, cayenne pepper, chili powder, paprika, thyme, onion powder, cumin, and garlic powder: (Combine the seasonings, to make a Cajun-style seasoning, with the right amount of spiciness for you!)

Side Dishes: Brown Rice and Seasonal Vegetables

1. Start cooking the brown rice. Preheat the oven to 400 degrees F. Rinse the tilapia and season it with olive oil, salt and pepper. Bake for 10 minutes in a glass casserole dish.

2. While baking, add the heavy whipping cream to a saucepan and barely bring to a boil. Add the minced garlic, seasonings to taste, lime juice, and cilantro. Grate the cheese into the sauce. Stir the sauce continuously, until it thickens slightly but don't overboil.

3. Remove the tilapia from the oven and cover it with the Spicy Cilantro Cream Sauce (you will have some sauce left). Return the tilapia to the oven for approximately 15 minutes or until the fish is done.

4. At this point, saute the vegetables in olive oil. We used minced garlic, sliced onion, and diced carrots plus a variety of baby greens from our garden.

5. Serve this entrée immediately once the fish is done and add some of the extra Spicy Cilantro Cream Sauce to the vegetables and rice. Garnish the tilapia with fresh cilantro.

Observing Lent

by Haley

This season of the Christian Year is represented by the color purple: the color of the bruised heart. This is the uncomfortable time preceding Easter when we remove distractions, focus on spiritual formation, and take an honest look at ourselves in order that we might prepare our hearts.

Consider incorporating these traditions during this season:

- **Cover crucifixes with purple fabric.** I let our preschooler find all the crucifixes and crosses in the house and help me do this on ~~Ash Wednesday.~~ *Passion Week*

- Display a "Crown of Thorns" grapevine wreath on your table.

- Attend daily Mass more frequently.

- Commit to a daily Rosary.

- Learn a new prayer.

- **Do Spiritual reading**. Spend time reading devotional texts and spiritual writings.

- **Look for ways to serve.** Find a way to give in your community. This might include making meals for new parents, visiting elderly parishioners, or sacrificing non-essentials in order to take up charitable giving.

- **Go to Confession.**

- **Go to Adoration or sign up for a Holy Hour.**

- **Go to Stations of the Cross hosted at your church or do them at your house and invite friends to join you.**

Lent: Cleaning Up Our Souls

by Haley

"I CAN'T do it! It's TOO HARD!" whined my three-year-old son, as he sat in the middle of his messy room. He burst into tears, at the prospect of cleaning up the toys, books, and stuffed animals scattered everywhere.

Maybe I'm asking too much, I thought. *He's clearly overwhelmed. Maybe he doesn't know where to start.*

"Why don't you just put the books on your shelf, to begin, and then we can figure out what to do next."

"Nooooo!" he cried. *"There's TOO MANY BOOKS. I CAN'T clean them ALL up!"*

OK," I sighed. *"How about this. Start with this Dr. Seuss book. Just grab it and set it on your bookshelf."*

"This is TOO HARD!" he complained. *"You do it!"*

Are you serious? I thought. *This is his mess. I told him exactly what to do. I'm in here helping him. All I'm asking is for him to make an attempt at doing his part. This is ridiculous!* I groaned.

Fast forward a couple of days: I'm praying during my holy hour, in the Chapel of Perpetual Adoration at our Parish. It's Lent. I'm tired and discouraged. It's just not going well. I am making no progress in cleaning up my messy soul. *"Lord, I just can't do it. It's too hard! I've got all this sin all over the place and I can't even begin to clean it up."*

Just start with one thing. Work on one small thing. Don't be overwhelmed.

"Ok, fine. But how do I even do it? How do I even start working on one thing?"

Prayer, Fasting, and Almsgiving. Ask me to help you, embrace spiritual discipline, sacrifice, and give.

"That's too much! I can't do all that!"

Well, why don't you just start with prayer?

"When would I have time for that?!"

Wake up ten minutes before your babies. Ask Me to help you with the one thing you want to focus on this Lent.

"Give up ten minutes of sleep?! Are You kidding me? Don't you know how tired I am? I'm never going to be able to clean this up! And You won't even help me! Waaaaaaaaaaa!"

Then I remembered my little boy's face, tears streaming down in frustration, his little fists clenched, instead of making even the smallest attempt to begin the task set before him. *Look familiar?* I closed my eyes and chuckled at myself. *That's me, right there, refusing to make the smallest gesture toward changing.* Because it's not any fun to clean up your soul. It's easier to say, *"I can't"* and just keep sitting in the muck. *You've told me exactly what I need to do to begin. You're right here helping me. And here I am, shaking my tiny fists in protest.*

How often do I respond to God's grace with absurd defiance? How often do I respond to God's plan, as my preschooler responds to disagreeable instructions: *"But, I don't WANT to."* As if that's a logical argument that gets me off the hook?

One of our daily household struggles is our twice-a-day application of coconut oil, to alleviate our son's eczema. *"I hate this!"* he screams and writhes. *"It doesn't feel good! Don't EVER do coconut oil again!"* How often do I push away God's grace because I'd rather carry on with a broken, raw soul, scratching at it until it bleeds, instead of participating in His plan to heal it? *"I can handle this just how it is! I don't mind having a diseased soul! Just don't ask me to get cleaned up, healed, and whole -- because I REALLY hate the process."*

But just as I love my son too much to let him scratch his skin raw, no matter the amount of kicking and screaming that results from applying a remedy, God loves us too much to let us be content to remain sick in our sin. This Lent, we can sit and whine about how hard it is to make any progress on this path to holiness, or we can recognize our messy sin, ask for God's grace and, with His help, start cleaning up. Let's jump in with both feet and ask Our Lord to help us.

March 23: St. Turibius of Mongrovejo

by Daniel

About the Saint

Turibius of Mongrovejo (1538-1606) was born into a noble family in Spain. First a professor of law, he later became a priest and was sent as a missionary to Peru. There, he became the Archbishop of Lima. St. Turibius was famous for traveling his diocese by foot, evangelizing, and baptizing the native people. Among the thousands of people that he baptized and confirmed are St. Rose of Lima and St. Martin de Porres. St. Turibius was a fierce defender of native people and is now the patron saint of native rights.

Lomo Saltado

Lomo Saltado is a popular Peruvian dish that showcases the unique fusion of Chinese and indigenous cuisine called "Chifa."

Ingredients

1 lb beef (flank or skirt steak) cut into strips

2 TBSP soy sauce

1 TBSP oil

1 red onion, sliced into strips

3 tomatoes, sliced

3 cloves garlic, minced

1 jalapeno, seeded and sliced

french fries*

salt, cumin, and paprika to taste

¼ cup chopped cilantro

*Making French fries is easy *if* you know how to do it: Scrub a couple of potatoes. Slice them into thin (¼ to ½ inch) strips. Soak them in cold water for an hour. Drain and pat dry. Heat vegetable oil or lard in a pot: Use enough to cover the bottom of the pot. Gently place the potato strips into the pot, being careful not to splash any of the hot oil. Turn the potato strips a couple of times and cook until golden and crispy -- about 5 minutes. Dry the potato strips on paper towels. Sprinkle the potato strips with salt. [If you're not comfortable making your own, frozen fries can work.]

1) Marinate the beef in the soy sauce, garlic, and salt (for at least 30 minutes -- but an hour or two is preferable).

2) Remove the beef from the marinade and sauté about a minute. Keep the marinade on hand. Add the onion to the meat and sauté for another minute. Add the tomato and pepper. Season with cumin and paprika. Add some of the marinade to this mixture as necessary to keep it from drying out. The vegetables should be cooked but not mushy.

3) Serve the meat on top of the French fries, with a side of white rice. Garnish with cilantro and top with Aiji sauce.

Aiji Sauce

Peruvian restaurants usually serve an amazing green, creamy, hot sauce made from Aiji, a yellow pepper popular in Peru. Everyone has a very different idea of how to make it, but this recipe produces a rich, cool sauce with a kick.

½ head iceberg lettuce

2 hot peppers, seeded (use Aiji peppers if you can find them. If not, substitute another variety. Also, add more or less peppers, to suit your heat tolerance.)

½ cup mayo

1 clove garlic

splash of vinegar

handful of cilantro

salt, pepper

1. Toss everything into a blender and puree until smooth. If you have sauce leftover, it will go well with eggs the next day.

"Time is not our own, and we must give strict account of it."
– St. Turibius of Mongrovejo

Eastertide

by Daniel

Before we observed Lent and Holy Week, Easter seemed to come out of nowhere. Palm Sunday popped up on the calendar, announcing Jesus was about to die. And then, one quiet week later, Jesus was risen (everything that happened during the week was, apparently, assumed)! Under this model, Easter is an understandably short holiday. Like Thanksgiving or July 4th, Easter is a single day so there's no point giving it more weight than the calendar calls for. Eat some candy, go to church, bake a ham, and then move on.

But when we began to observe Lent, our view of the Easter season began to change. We realized Easter *doesn't* just come out of nowhere. It's the triumphal celebration after a long and sometimes difficult season.

Through Lent we wait and fast and wait. For forty days we think on the words *"Remember, oh man, that you are dust and to dust you shall return."* We pray, repent, and contemplate our need for Jesus. We descend into the darkness of Holy Week, watching again as Christ is betrayed, remembering our own part in his death as we shout with the crowd, *"Crucify him!"* We wait through a bleak Holy Saturday for the Easter vigil to finally come and when it does we rejoice! Christ is risen!

After all of this, Easter *can't* be just one day! And, fortunately, the Easter season goes on for 50 more days! Eastertide is the season from the Easter Vigil all the way to Pentecost. Saint Athanasius called this huge feast, the "great Lord's Day." During this season, we celebrate Christ's resurrection and get ready to remember the coming of the Holy Spirit at Pentecost. So celebrate! Feast! Maybe you can't have a ham every single day (or CAN you?!) but you can mark the time as special. This is especially important for the Sundays of Easter and the first eight days of Easter, called the Octave. Maybe this means a special dessert, a colorful salad, or a nice bottle of wine. The important thing is to remember, *"He is risen indeed!"*

Easter Nasturtium Salad

This Easter salad is a mix of spring greens and nasturtiums, an edible flower.

Easter Prayer of St. Hippolytus of Rome

Christ is Risen: The world below lies desolate
Christ is Risen: The spirits of evil are fallen
Christ is Risen: The angels of God are rejoicing
Christ is Risen: The tombs of the dead are empty
Christ is Risen indeed from the dead, the first of the sleepers,
Glory and power are His forever and ever
-St. Hippolytus (AD 190-236)

April 23: St. George

by Haley

About the Saint

St. George was a brave Christian and Roman soldier. When the Emperor Diocletian began persecuting Christians, St. George left his position in the Emperor's army. As a result, the authorities tortured and beheaded him. Artistic images of St. George often depict him slaying a dragon and rescuing a maiden; there are many legends about St. George with this motif. The dragon represents the evil that St. George courageously fought and the maiden signifies the truth of the Gospel that he upheld. He is the patron saint of England.

Haley's Shepherd's Pie

If I have a culinary claim to fame, it's this Shepherd's Pie recipe. I started to make it for friends in need of comfort food, and now it's the requested meal whenever a friend has a new baby. A friend confessed that it's so good that she started eating it straight out of the pan. I always make a double or triple recipe because my older brother will inevitably "stop by to say hello," when he hears that it's in the oven. And it's the perfect meal to celebrate St. George of Merry England!

Ingredients

(For the filling)

1 lb. ground beef (or lamb, if you want to be authentic!)

1 onion, diced

1-2 cloves garlic, minced

5 carrots, chopped

3 stalks of celery, chopped

2 cups of frozen peas

2 TBSP all-purpose flour (or arrowroot powder, to make it gluten-free)

1 tsp ground cinnamon

½ tsp ground cloves

½ tsp ground ginger

2 TBSP fresh parsley, chopped

1 TBSP fresh oregano, chopped (you can substitute dried oregano)

1 & ½ cups beef broth

salt and pepper, to taste

(For the mashed potato topping)

5-6 potatoes, chopped (I don't bother peeling them, if they're organic, but peel them first, if you don't like skins in your mashed potatoes)

½ cup butter (this amount makes them delicious – but you may use less)

1 cup milk

4 oz. cream cheese

salt and pepper, to taste

shredded cheddar cheese to generously sprinkle on top

1) Preheat the oven to 400 degrees F.

2) Sauté the ground beef in a large pot, until partially browned (5 minutes).

3) Add onion, garlic, carrot, and celery: Sauté until the onion begins to brown. Add peas and stir.

4) Mix in the flour (or arrowroot powder), spices, and herbs.

5) Add the beef broth to the mixture and add salt and pepper to taste.

6) Simmer for 15 minutes. Stir occasionally. Almost all the liquid should be absorbed.

7) Pour the filling into a large oven-safe casserole dish.

8) Boil potatoes in water, until tender (15-25 minutes, depending how small you chopped them).

9) Drain the potatoes and mash until smooth (I use my KitchenAid mixer to whip them). Add butter, cream cheese, milk, and salt and pepper to taste.

10) Spread the mashed potatoes over the filling and sprinkle cheese on top.

11) Bake in the oven for 30 minutes (or until the cheese is bubbly and golden brown.)

St. George, pray for us!

May 21: Feast of the Mexican Martyrs

by Daniel

About the Saints

In the 1920s, Mexican President Elias Calles began enforcing brutal anti-Catholic laws. Priests who ignored the laws were fined, arrested, and even killed. Soon, many Catholics rebelled against the government, beginning the three year Cristero War. Thousands of federal troops, rebels, and civilians were killed and the cruel treatment of priests and laypeople at the hands of the government deepened. Blessed Pope John Paul II canonized 25 saints from this period, most of them priests who did not take up arms but continued to carry out their ministry in the face of persecution and death. This feast day is a reminder that religious persecution is not relegated to a distant time or a distant land. Still, more importantly, we celebrate the courage, faithfulness, and selflessness of these saints.

Rajas con Crema

This is a popular dish in central and southern Mexico that can be served at breakfast or dinner and eaten as a side dish or a main course with beans and eggs. Poblano peppers are best but bell peppers will work just fine (especially if your garden overflows with them like ours does!).

Ingredients

6 large peppers (poblanos or bell)

½ large onion cut into strips

1 TBSP of butter

½ cup sour cream

½ cup milk

½ cup cheese (Monterey jack or cheddar)

salt

1. Char the peppers on all sides. The best way to do this is over the open flame of a gas stovetop. Just set them on the grate and turn them with tongs. Let them get nice and black. You can do this in an oven on broil if you have to, but an open flame is best. And more fun!

2. Let the peppers cool then use your fingers to peel off the charred skin. The blackened parts will come off easily. You can run the peppers under water quickly if you need to.

3. Remove the tops and seeds from the peppers and then cut them into thin strips.

4. Heat the butter in a skillet and add the sliced onion. After a few minutes, toss in the peppers and add a bit of salt. Stir and cook for a minute. Then add the sour cream and milk, simmer for another three or four minutes. The peppers should be soft but not mushy. Remove from heat, add the cheese and stir.

5. Serve with warm tortillas.

Saints of the Cristero War, pray for us!

May 22: St. Michael Ho-Dinh-Hy

by Daniel

Michael Ho-Dinh-Hy was a wealthy silk trader and powerful mandarin in the Vietnamese Empire. Although he was born into a Christian family, St. Michael did not openly practice his faith until later in life. He helped many Christian missionaries working in Vietnam which was illegal. Ho-Dinh-Hy was arrested, tortured, and publicly beheaded. In 1990, St. Michael Ho-Dinh-Hy was canonized along with 116 Vietnamese martyrs.

Vietnamese Peanut Sauce

May is a time of transition here in North Florida. We're at the very end of our Winter and early Spring season but not yet in full production for late Spring and Summer. So we usually have a little lettuce and a few radishes and onions left but only the beginnings of tomatoes and peppers on the vine. This meal is the perfect opportunity for us to enjoy the last of our lettuce before it bolts or wilts under our hot sun. I used to work at a Vietnamese restaurant and, after a busy lunch, the owner would prepare something simple like this before the dinner rush began. It doesn't get much simpler than a fried egg over fresh greens with a splash of peanut dressing. This dressing can also double as a dipping sauce for many South Asian foods.

Ingredients

⅔ cup crunchy peanut butter

⅓ cup water

1 TBSP soy sauce

1 TBSP sesame oil or vegetable oil

1 TBSP sugar

Splash of sriracha sauce

1. Mix all ingredients until smooth. Add more liquid if necessary.

2. Pour peanut sauce over fresh greens and serve with a fried egg.

3. Store extra sauce in the fridge.

St. Michael Ho-Dinh-Hy, pray for us!

June 3: St. Charles Lwanga and Companions

by Daniel

About the Saints

Charles Lwanga served as the major-domo to the king of Buganda, a kingdom in what is now southern Uganda. As missionaries began to convert many people to Christianity, the king perceived this as the attempt of foreign governments to infiltrate and subvert his authority, so he ordered all the new Christians to revert.

When the Christians refused to revert, the king ordered their execution. Because of St. Charles Lwanga's high rank, persecutors singled him out and ordered a separate execution by fire. As the flames consumed him, he told his executioner, "It is as if you are pouring water on me.

Please repent and become a Christian like me." Many of St. Charles Lwanga's companions were burned that day. The authorities tortured and killed nearly 100 Christians, Catholic and Anglican, before the persecutions ceased.

Ugali with African Chicken Stew

Called "posho" in many parts of Uganda, ugali is a staple of eastern and southern African cuisine. It's simply a mixture of corn flour and water, cooked to a smooth, almost dough-like consistency. The traditional way to eat ugali is to take a piece and use it as a kind of utensil, to scoop up meat and vegetables.

Ingredients (Ugali)

2 cups corn flour

4 cups water

salt to taste

butter (optional)

1) Bring the water to a boil

2) Add the corn flour a little at a time, mixing constantly. Mash out any lumps.

3) If you're a Southerner, you'll notice the similarity of ugali to grits and you simply won't be able to stop yourself from adding butter and salt. Go for it. If you're not a Southerner and don't know what I'm talking about, don't worry.

4) Keep stirring! The more you stir, the better consistency you'll achieve. If you need to, add more corn flour to thicken.

African Chicken Stew

4 chicken thighs

3 TBSP olive oil

1 large yellow onion, diced (¾ for the stew and ¼ for the sauce, below)

2 sweet potatoes, chopped into cubes

3 cloves of garlic, diced

1 TBSP curry powder (coriander, turmeric, cumin, cloves, cinnamon, dried chili, powdered ginger)

1 [14-oz] can of diced tomatoes

1 cup chicken broth

1 TBSP cornstarch

salt

1) Heat oil in a pot and brown the chicken thighs, over medium high heat. Add the onion (only ¾ if you're also making the peanut sauce) and cook, until softened.

2) Add the garlic and sweet potatoes. Cook for a few minutes. Add the tomatoes and curry powder. Stir and cook another 2-3 minutes. Add the chicken broth. Turn the heat down and simmer until the chicken is tender enough to fall off the bone.

3) Remove the chicken and strip the meat from the bones. Add the cornstarch to the pot and stir. Pull the chicken apart and return to the pot. Serve the stew with ugali and peanut sauce. This also goes well with a vegetable side, like sauteed greens and peppers.

Peanut Sauce

¼ diced onion

2 TBSP olive oil

½ cup peanut butter

½ cup water

2 tsp paprika

salt

1) Fry the onions in the oil, until soft.

2) Turn the heat off and add the peanut butter and the paprika. Mix together with the onions. Add the water, as needed, to form a thick sauce.

Martyrs of Uganda, pray for us!

July 6: St. Maria Goretti

by Daniel

About the Saint

St. Maria Goretti was a young Italian girl, a virgin-martyr, who became the patron saint of young women and of purity. A man named Alexander intended to have sex with her. She refused, warning him what he wanted to do was sinful. Alexander was undeterred and attempted to rape her. Maria fought back and was stabbed multiple times. She later forgave him for his crime. She died from the injuries from that assault.

When serving time in prison, Alexander, formerly unrepentant, had a dream of Maria, which transformed his life. He sought forgiveness from Maria's family and was present when she was canonized in 1950.

Simplified Pasta Pescatore

Two staples of Southern Italian cuisine are tomatoes and seafood. Marinara actually means "mariner's." One popular dish, along the coasts of Italy, is Pasta Pescatore, "fisherman's pasta." There are many variations but the basic idea is seafood, in tomato sauce, over pasta. If you have access to fresh, high quality seafood, please make use of it. Shrimp, mussels, scallops, and a variety of fish would all work wonderfully. This is SIMPLIFIED, though, so we just used frozen tilapia filets.

Ingredients

2 TBSP extra-virgin olive oil

1/2 onion, diced

3 cloves garlic, minced

1/2 cup dry white wine

3 banana peppers, optional

2 cups diced fresh tomatoes (or canned)

1 tsp red pepper flakes

1 handful of fresh oregano and fresh thyme, chopped

1 handful fresh basil, chopped

2 tilapia fillets, thawed and cut into chunks

Cooked pasta

*A note on tomatoes: For this recipe, we used fresh tomatoes because we have them in abundance. The flavor, in a sauce like this, is very light and perfect for summer. You should probably peel and remove the seeds first but that's a lot of effort! Canned tomatoes will certainly be acceptable but the flavor will be quite different.

1. In a large skillet, heat the onion in the olive oil until it begins to soften. Then add the banana peppers (if using) and garlic. Continue sautéing.

2. Add the wine, tomatoes, oregano, and thyme. If using fresh tomatoes, let them break down for a few minutes.

3. Add the seafood and cook, until done. For tilapia, this should only take a few minutes.

4. Serve over pasta, with the chopped basil tossed on top. You can also sprinkle this dish with grated cheese. Bread would also be nice to soak up the extra sauce.

St. Maria Goretti, pray for us!

— Feast! © Daniel and Haley Stewart 2013

July 9: St. Augustine Zhao Rong and 119 Companions

by Daniel

About the Saints

Augustine Zhao Rong was a soldier who escorted a Catholic Bishop, Monsignor Dufresse, to Beijing to be executed. Moved by the bishop's willingness to be martyred, Augustine became a Christian and entered seminary. Once a priest, he was arrested, tortured and killed. The 119 companions were martyred between 1648 to 1930.

Chinese Christians have suffered intense persecution since the middle of the 17th century. This persecution perhaps reached its peak in the 1930s during the Boxer Rebellion when over 30,000 Christians were killed. The danger for our Chinese brothers and sisters continues today under an oppressive communist government. Please pray for the Christians in China and ask for the intercession of the brave saints we celebrate today.

Fried Rice

An incredibly versatile dish, fried rice can be made with a near infinite combination of vegetables, meats, and herbs. We make it year round with whatever happens to be in the garden or leftover in the fridge. We often make an egg-based version for breakfast as well. Tomatoes, peas, carrots, onions, and greens can all be tossed in. This particular recipe is from the middle of our summer growing season. Feel free to make major adjustments! I find one- or two-day-old rice works the best. We usually make extra rice for another meal and save some for fried rice.

Ingredients

3 eggs

2 TBSP vegetable oil

2 bell peppers, diced

2 handfuls of green beans, chopped

2 cloves of garlic, diced

12 shrimp, peeled

3 cups cooked rice

1 TBSP soy sauce

1 handful of basil, roughly chopped

salt and pepper

1) Heat 1 tablespoon of oil in a wok or large skillet. Toss in the green beans, bell peppers, and garlic. Cook until the vegetables just begin to

soften. Add the shrimp and stir until they're cooked through. Remove the vegetables and shrimp, set aside.

2) Scramble the eggs in the wok until cooked, set aside. Clean out the pan if necessary.

3) Add another tablespoon of oil to the wok. Add the rice, stir and break up any clumps. Add the soy sauce and stir. Cook the rice until it begins to turn just a little crispy. Return all the other ingredients back to the wok along with the basil. Stir until everything is mixed together. Season with salt and pepper. Serve immediately.

Martyr Saints of China, pray for us!

July 26: Sts. Anne and Joachim

by Daniel

About the Saints

St. Anne and St. Joachim are the mother and father of the Blessed Virgin Mary and also the grandparents of Our Lord. Having been barren for 20 years, St. Anne gave birth to the Blessed Virgin, at the age of 40. Her Hebrew name, Hanna, is the same as Hannah in the Old Testament and their stories mirror one another.

According to tradition, angels [separately] told St. Anne and St. Joachim (ages 40 and 69) they were pregnant with a daughter who would be consecrated to God. There are beautiful artistic renderings of the moment that they see each other, after the good news, and kiss and hug each other. They are both the patron saints of parents and grandparents and St. Anne is also the patron saint of homemakers and women in labor.

Moules Marinières

Shellfish is a traditional food to prepare on St. Anne's Day and this dish (Mariner's Mussels) is from Brittany, a region particularly devoted to St. Anne.

Ingredients

1 lb mussels in the shell

1 lb shrimp

3 TBSP butter

1 onion, finely chopped

3 cloves garlic, minced

1 cup white wine (Muscadet would be most authentic but Sauvignon Blanc will work fine)

¼ cup parsley, finely chopped

1 large or 2-3 small tomatoes, diced

salt and pepper – to taste

1. Peel the shrimp and wash the mussels, scrubbing them to remove the "beard," the fine white filaments on the outside of the shell.

2. Heat the butter in a large pot. Sauté the onions and garlic, until the onions are translucent. Stir in the tomato and parsley. Add the mussels, shrimp, and wine, stirring gently, so as not to break the shells.

3. Cover the pot and let it steam for 4-5 minutes. Uncover to stir every minute, so that the shrimp will cook evenly. Season to taste with salt and pepper. Remove from heat and make sure to save the sauce to dip bread in. (Technically, Moules Marinières should be just mussels but we also added shrimp, for those who aren't fond of mussels.)

Serving suggestions

On St. Anne's feast day, girls named after St. Anne traditionally wore red and green ribbons in their hair. Serve a salad made with arugula and lettuce, with tomatoes, for the red and green effect. And you can serve the Moules Marinières over sliced baguette, with roasted potatoes.

And you might want to invite some grandparents, over since St. Anne and St. Joachim are the patron saints of grandparents!

Sts. Anne and Joachim, pray for us!

August 23: St. Rose of Lima

by Daniel

About the Saint

St. Rose was the first saint from the Americas. She was born in Lima, Peru and showed great holiness from an early age. She modeled her spiritual practice after St. Catherine of Siena by fasting three times a week and taking on other secret and severe penances. To discourage suitors and to guard against vanity, she cut her hair short and disfigured her face with lye. When she was 20, she joined the Dominicans and committed great acts of love throughout her life. Her holiness grew and she continued fasting and self-mortification, until she died at the age of 31. In addition to her home city of Lima, St. Rose is also the patroness of Latin America, the Philippines, embroiderers, and the resolution of family quarrels.

Pancit Bihon

For a few months after high school, I lived in the Philippines where I worked on sustainable agriculture projects. One of my favorite meals was Pancit. It is one of those wonderful comfort foods that you can never recreate exactly how you remember it. Also, the ingredient list is extremely versatile. I remember walking to one of the little shops that stood along the mountain roads to buy the noodles, one little baggy of soy sauce, one little baggy of oil, a pepper, an onion, and a can of corned beef hash. I sat around a small table with a dozen other people, sharing a huge bowl of Pancit, a huge bowl of rice, and several glass bottles of warm soda. I doubt that I'll ever be able to recreate that taste experience.

Ingredients

1 lb chicken - cut into small pieces and marinated in the soy sauce

½ lb shrimp, peeled

1 small onion, diced

2 banana peppers, diced

3 cloves garlic, minced

2 or 3 carrots, thinly sliced

2 TBSP oil (canola or vegetable)

1 TBSP soy sauce

1 splash of fish sauce

2 packages of rice vermicelli noodles (6 oz each)

2 cups baby spinach

A few sprigs of cilantro

Ground pepper and soy sauce, to taste

1) Stir fry the onions and garlic in 1 tbsp oil, over medium heat in a wok or big sauté pan. After 1 or 2 minutes, add the carrots, peppers, and chicken. When the chicken is almost done, add the shrimp. Once the meat is cooked through, set all of those ingredients aside.

2) Soak the dry noodles in warm water for about 15-20 minutes until they soften. Place the noodles in boiling water for a few minutes and drain.

3) Place the noodles in the wok and add the cooked ingredients back, along with the spinach, cilantro, soy sauce, and ground pepper. Stir everything together.

4) Serve with rice and warm soda. Just kidding about the soda.

"Apart from the Cross, there is no other ladder by which we may get to Heaven."- St. Rose of Lima

August 31: St Raymond Nonnatus

by Daniel

About the Saint

St. Raymond Nonnatus was born in Catalonia, Spain. His mother died during childbirth, so Raymond was delivered via Cesarean section (hence, the epithet Nonnatus, Latin for "not born"). And if you watch the BBC series, *Call the Midwife*, now you know why the midwives live at "Nonnatus House!"

He became a member of the Mercedarian Order, whose mission was to ransom Christian prisoners from the Muslim Moors in North Africa. Raymond succeeded the order's founder, St. Peter Nolasco, as the master-general who was responsible for traveling to Africa to ransom the captives. When St. Raymond ran out of money, he offered himself as a hostage, taking the place of one of the prisoners.

In prison, he continued to work for the advancement of the Kingdom of God and won many converts to the Christian faith. No amount of torture or punishment could keep St. Raymond from preaching the gospel -- so his captors bored holes through his lips and padlocked them shut.

At one point, Raymond received a sentence of death. However, his captors kept him alive, in the hope of receiving a large ransom, in exchange for his life. He was later returned to Spain and died near Barcelona. He is the patron saint of expectant mothers, midwives, newborns, and falsely-accused people.

Catalan Picada Chicken

This is one of our all-time favorite recipes! Picada (not to be confused with the Italian "picatta") is a paste used to thicken and add depth of flavor to an entrée. Somewhat similar to a molé -- but without the heat -- picada is a distinctive aspect of Catalan cuisine. There are probably as many recipes for picada as there are abuelas in Catalonia, but this is a basic recipe to draw from.

Ingredients

4 chicken breasts

2 & ½ TBSP extra-virgin olive oil

1 medium onion, diced

1 [14-ounce] can diced tomatoes

1 cup chicken broth

¼ cup Spanish red wine, such as Rioja

1 [3-inch] strip of orange zest

¼ tsp fresh thyme leaves

For the Picada

1 slice of thickly-crusted bread, cut into ½ inch cubes (yield: ½ cup)*

¼ cup whole almonds

3 garlic cloves, coarsely-chopped and sautéed

1 ounce bittersweet chocolate, chopped

¼ cup fresh chopped parsley

$^1/_8$ ground cinnamon

¼ tsp ground cumin

pinch of ground cloves

salt and pepper, to taste

*(You may substitute gluten-free bread, if necessary.)

1) Toast the bread and almonds in a 350 F degree oven until the bread begins to brown. Transfer the bread and almonds to a food processor. Add the chocolate, parsley, garlic, cinnamon, cumin, and cloves. Blend these ingredients together, adding olive oil and wine, until it yields a thick paste.

2) Season the chicken with salt and pepper, to taste. In a large skillet, heat 2 tablespoons of the oil. Add the chicken breasts and cook over moderately high heat, until browned. Transfer the chicken to a plate and cut into pieces.

3) Add the onion to the skillet and cook, over moderate heat, until softened. Add the tomatoes and thyme and cook for 5 minutes. Add the broth, sherry, and orange zest and bring to a boil. Add the chicken, cover and simmer over low heat for 15 minutes, turning once.

4) Stir the picada into the sauce and simmer, over low heat, for 15 minutes. You will end up with a thick, extremely rich sauce.

5) Season the entrée with salt and pepper and serve over rice or with toasted bread. Because of the depth of flavor in the picada, this dish goes well with simple vegetables. We chose peppers and green beans, tossed in olive oil and roasted.

St. Raymond Nonnatus, pray for us!

September 5: Blessed Teresa of Calcutta

by Daniel

About the Saint

Blessed Teresa of Calcutta, often called Mother Teresa, was the founder of the Missionaries of Charity. She was born in Albania and at age 18, Blessed Teresa joined the Sisters of Loreto in India, teaching at the convent school. She later received permission from the Vatican to found the Missionaries of Charity which serves "the hungry, the naked, the homeless, the crippled, the blind, the lepers, all those people who feel unwanted, unloved, uncared for throughout society, people that have become a burden to the society and are shunned by everyone." She spent her life serving the poorest of the poor.

Garden Fresh Curry

This simple curry is easily adaptable to what's in season or what you have an abundance of in your garden. Green beans, squash, and okra would all be excellent additions. For protein, we used eggs because of how abundant they are for us right now. One can of chickpeas would be a good substitute.

Ingredients

1 large eggplant peeled and cut into chunks

1 large bell pepper or 3-4 banana peppers, diced

1 onion diced

2 cloves of garlic minced

5 medium tomatoes diced (about 2 cups)

½ TBSP curry powder (we make our own with cumin, tumeric, corriander, and paprika).

½ cup yogurt

4 hardboiled eggs cut in half

1 handful of fresh basil chopped

oil

salt

1) In a wok or wide saucepan, fry the diced onion in the oil until it begins to soften. Add the peppers, garlic, eggplant, and curry powder. Stir and then let cook for about 3 minutes.

2) Add the tomatoes and stir. Add 1 cup of water and bring to a boil. Let the water cook down and the eggplant soften (it should be soft but not at all mushy). You may need to add a little more water to prevent the vegetables from sticking but you don't want too much water or things will become soupy.

3) Once the eggplant is ready, stir in the yogurt. Then the basil. Then, gently, the already boiled eggs.

4) Serve with rice and garnish with more basil. Naan or other Indian breads would also go well with this versatile curry.

Blessed Mother Teresa of Calcutta, pray for us!

September 29: The Feast of the Archangels (Michaelmas)

by Daniel and Haley

About the Feast

When we first became drawn to observing the Christian Year, Michaelmas was the first feast we celebrated. Pronounced "Mickel-mas," this feast day celebrates the Archangels. It follows the fall Ember Days during which Christians traditionally thanked God for his creation and the bounty of the earth and fasted penitentially. Michaelmas was a Holy Day of Obligation until the 18th century and honors St. Michael, St. Gabriel, and St. Raphael.

In Hebrew, the name Michael means "Who Is Like God?" It is a rhetorical question, of course, because no one is like God. The word is also the battle cry of the angels. St. Michael fought against Lucifer and the fallen angels and defended the friends of God. You probably remember that St.

Gabriel announced the coming of Jesus to the Virgin Mary and also the coming of John the Baptist to Zachariah. St. Raphael is found in the book of Tobit.

Celebrate with Flowers

The aster flower, also known as the Michaelmas Daisy is in season in North America at the end of September. Grow some in your garden, or purchase daisies to grace your Michaelmas table.

"The Michaelmas daisies, among dede weeds,
Bloom for St Michael's valorous deeds.
And seems the last of flowers that stood,
Till the feast of St. Simon and St. Jude."

Roast Michaelmas Chicken

Goose is the traditional Michaelmas fowl and if you can get your hands on one for a reasonable price, you absolutely should. But, around here, geese seem to be quite expensive, so we go with the more affordable cousin of the goose; the chicken. This bird is roasted with apple and sage to give it a Michaelmas flavor.

Ingredients

1 whole chicken, (5-6 lbs)

4 TBSP butter, softened

1 TBSP each of fresh rosemary, sage, and thyme, minced

salt and pepper

2 small apples, cored and quartered

2 small onions (or one large), peeled and quartered

extra sprigs of rosemary, sage, and thyme

1) Preheat the oven to 425 degrees F. Mix the minced herbs, salt and pepper into the softened butter.

2) Remove the giblets from inside the chicken. At the front and back of the chicken, work your finger between the skin and meat, it should separate easily. Spoon the butter mixture under the skin and work it across the breast and back until you have an even coating between the skin and meat. This may take a little practice but will ensure a crispy skin and more flavorful meat than if you just rub the butter on the outside. Rub the remaining butter over the wings, legs, and any difficult to reach spots.

3) Stuff the chicken with the herb sprigs and half of the onions and apples. Place the rest of the apples and onions on the bottom of a roasting pan and place the chicken on top. This will keep the chicken out of its juice so the skin can get crispy.

4) Roast the chicken for about 1 ½ hours. The skin should be golden brown and the juices should run clear when pierced with a knife. Use a meat thermometer to make sure the breast meat is 180 degrees.

5) Remove the chicken from the oven and let it rest 10 minutes before carving. Serve with the apples and onions, mashed turnips, and steamed carrots.

Mashed Turnips

Here's the secret to making any vegetable absolutely delicious: butter. Turnips get a bad rap, but they're nutritious and really quite tasty.

Ingredients

7 turnips, peeled and cut into cubes

3 TBSP butter

½ cup milk

salt and pepper

1) Boil the cubed turnips in salted water until they're soft and tender, about 20-30 minutes.

2) Mash turnips until smooth like you would potatoes. We used our KitchenAid. Blend in the milk and butter. Salt and pepper to taste.

Other Suggestions

Carrots are a very traditional food for Michaelmas. According to a Scottish custom, women would harvest wild carrots on Michaelmas by digging triangular holes with a three-pronged mattock. Apparently the holes represent St. Michael's shield and the mattock represents his trident. A simple bread called St. Michael's Bannock and blackberries are also traditional. There's a legend concerning Lucifer falling into a blackberry bush after being expelled from heaven by St. Michael and spitting on the blackberries to make them bitter so that they cannot be picked after Michaelmas.

On Michaelmas Day the devil puts his foot on the blackberries.
-Irish Proverb

Prayer to St. Michael the Archangel

St. Michael the Archangel, defend us in battle. Be our defense against the wickedness and snares of the Devil. May God rebuke him, we humbly pray, and do thou, O Prince of the heavenly hosts, by the power of God, thrust into hell Satan, and all the evil spirits, who prowl about the world seeking the ruin of souls. Amen.

October 10: St. Francis Borgia

by Daniel

About the Saint

St. Francis Borgia, the 4th Duke of Grandía, was born to a wealthy, noble family in Valencia, Spain. He and his wife, Eleanor, had eight children. Despite his wealth and power, St. Francis and his family lived a pious life and were devoted to Christ and His Church. After the death of his wife, Francis renounced his titles, in favor of his son, and decided to become a Jesuit priest. Although he received offers of special treatment because of his high birth, he always refused them. Instead, he became renowned for his humility and his powerful preaching. Eventually, he received the appointment of the Superior General of the Society of Jesus. He sent missionaries all over the world and advised kings and popes, all while remaining humble and pious. He is a model of servant leadership — a virtue especially important to our contemporary society.

Simple Spanish Tapas

Simple Spanish Tapas are a delightful way to celebrate the last of the summer harvest (which continues here through late September and early October, where we live, in North Florida). The Spanish, like the Italians, appreciate the pleasure of fresh and unadulterated ingredients.

So, the first thing you're going to want to do is slice some fresh tomatoes, drizzle a little olive oil on top, and serve them with bread and a Spanish cheese, like Manchego. Do this first! That way you can eat, while you're making everything else.

Spanish Eggplant Spread

Ingredients

2 medium-sized eggplants, skinned and cut into ½ inch slices

2 cloves of garlic, roughly chopped

A few green onions, roughly chopped

1 handful of fresh parsley, chopped

olive oil

vinegar

salt and pepper

1) In a large skillet, saute the eggplant in olive oil, until the slices are thick and starting to brown. Then, set them aside.

2) Next, quickly saute the garlic and green onions.

3) Toss all three of these ingredients into a blender or food processor and add the parsley. Add a splash of olive oil, a splash of vinegar, and a dash of salt and pepper.

4) Blend together until smooth, adding more olive oil and vinegar, as necessary. Serve with warm bread.

Potatoes Aioli

3 medium potatoes, diced

2 banana peppers, diced

2 TBSP oil or lard

salt and pepper

1) Heat the oil in a large skillet and cook the potatoes over high heat. Stir frequently, to keep them from sticking.

2) Once the potatoes begin to soften, toss in the peppers. If things begin to stick, add a little more oil.

3) The potatoes are done once they are brown on the outside and soft on the inside. Top with the Aioli sauce [see below] and diced parsley.

Aioli Sauce

Aioli is basically garlic mayonnaise. The ratio is different but it's the same idea. So, you can find a trustworthy recipe and spend a long time whisking egg yolks and mixing everything just right OR you can do this:

Ingredients

½ cup mayo

olive oil

lemon juice

1 clove garlic, crushed

chili powder

1) Add a little oil, lemon juice, chili powder, and garlic to the mayo and whisk together. You want it to have more of a liquid consistency so that you can pour it on top of the potatoes.

2) All of this will go great with a crisp, pale ale or with red Spanish wine.

St. Francis Borgia, pray for us!

October 17: St. Ignatius of Antioch

by Daniel

There is one Physician who is possessed both of flesh and spirit; both made and not made; God existing in flesh; true life in death; both of Mary and of God; first passible and then impassible, even Jesus Christ our Lord. — St. Ignatius, *Letter to the Ephesians*

About the Saint

A student of St. John the Apostle, St. Ignatius became the third Bishop of Antioch and an important Church Father. At the turn of the century, he was arrested and sent away from Syria to Rome, to be executed. Along the way, he penned many letters that have survived and which give us invaluable insight into the work and theology of the first-century Christians. He wrote passionately regarding the deity and humanity of Christ; the authority of the bishop; and the importance of the Eucharist, which he called "the flesh of our Savior Jesus Christ." He also wrote of his complete willingness to suffer a marty's death, for the sake of Jesus. When he reached Rome, the authorities took him to the Colosseum, where wild animals killed him.

Despite over a millennium of Muslim rule, Christians still have a presence in Syria. However, during the brutal civil war, Syrian Christians have suffered, witnessing the destruction of their churches and the murders of many priests. Vast numbers of Syrian Christians have been driven from their homes. At the time of publishing, the war still rages on. On this feast day, please remember the Syrian Christians and all others suffering from the effects of this civil war. Ask especially for the intercession of St. Ignatius.

Mujaddara

This simple rice and lentil dish is popular in much of the Middle East, though it bears the unfortunate name, "mujaddara," literally "small pox." Supposedly, it's called that because the lentils look like little pock marks -- but I don't know for sure. I *do* know it tastes great, is easy to make, and our kids love it. Caramelized onions give this dish a fantastic sweet flavor that goes well with cinnamon and other spices.

Ingredients

2 cups basmati rice, cooked and set aside (should yield about 6 cups)

2 cups green/brown lentils

2 large onions, diced

4 TBSP olive oil

freshly-cracked pepper

2 tsp cumin

1 tsp cinnamon

1 tsp paprika

salt

1) Pour the lentils into a pot and cover with water, by at least one inch. Bring to a boil and then reduce the heat to a simmer. The lentils should be tender but not mushy. This will take about 15-20 minutes. Drain and set aside.

2) Heat the 2 tablespoons of olive oil in a large pan, over medium heat. Crack some freshly-cracked pepper into the oil. Add the onions and let them cook, stirring often, for 5-10 minutes, until they begin to "sweat" and lose some of their moisture. At this point, turn up the heat and stop stirring. Let the onions brown, until some of the smaller pieces begin to turn crispy. Remove from heat and turn them out onto a paper towel.

3) In a large bowl, mix together the lentils, rice, spices, the extra 2 tablespoons of olive oil, and most of the onions (set some aside to put on top of the entree). Serve with cucumber salad and hummus.

Cucumber and Yogurt Salad

1 cucumber, skinned and diced

2 cups plain yogurt

½ teaspoon cumin

1 dozen or so fresh mint leaves, chopped

splash of lemon juice

salt and fresh pepper

Mix all ingredients and serve chilled, either on the side or on top of the mujaddara.

Hummus

Ingredients

2 cups cooked chickpeas

2 TBSP tahini

2 garlic cloves, roughly chopped

3 TBSP olive oil

4 TBSP water

½ lemon

paprika, salt, and pepper

*Note on chickpeas: We soak and cook dry chickpeas. The required 2 cups of chickpeas in this recipe translates to about one can.

1. Add everything except the water to a food processor or blender. A food processor can achieve a smoother hummus but a blender can get the job done. Blend the ingredients, adding the water as necessary, until the hummus achieves the desired smoothness. We like a chunkier hummus but some people like it almost creamy.

2. Serve the hummus topped with a splash of olive oil and paprika.

"I am the wheat of Christ, ground by the teeth of beasts, to become pure bread." – St. Ignatius of Antioch's words at his martyrdom

November 11: St. Martin of Tours (Martinmas)

by Haley

About the Saint

While riding on his horse one day, St. Martin of Tours, a soldier in the Roman army, encountered a beggar. In order to clothe the poor man, Martin tore his own military cloak into two pieces and gave one half to the beggar. He then dreamed that Jesus was wearing the cloak and telling the angels that Martin had clothed him. Crescent-shaped pastries representing the horseshoes of St. Martin's horse are traditional for Martinmas and many regions also celebrate with lanterns.

Stuffed Butternut Squash

This is one of our favorite fall meals to prepare for special occasions. We serve it in halves (just like St. Martin's cloak).

Ingredients

2 butternut squash

1 lb sausage (we like to use pork breakfast sausage)

1 sweet onion, diced

3 carrots, diced

2 apples, diced

2 cloves garlic

1 & ½ cups breadcrumbs (we use gluten-free)

½ cup raisins

2 TBSP plain yogurt

2 TBSP fresh sage and rosemary (You may also add thyme or oregano. Use dried herbs if you don't have fresh herbs.)

1) Cut squash in half. (Because they're hard on the outside, this is a difficult task. I recommend that you microwave the butternut for a minute or two or bake it in the oven for 15 minutes, to make the job easier.)

2) Scoop out the seeds and the stringy parts around the seeds. (Save the seeds, if you want to roast them: See instructions below.)

3) Bake the squash in the oven at 350°F on a greased baking sheet (cut side down) until barely soft. (The baking time depends on the size of the squash but I usually bake mine for 40 minutes, before I check them to see if they're almost tender.)

4) In the meantime, brown the sausage. Add onion, apples, carrots, and garlic and sauté with the sausage for 5 minutes. (Add olive oil or butter, if needed.)

5) Add 1/4 cup water, cover, and let simmer for 5-10 minutes. Then, turn off the heat.

6) Add the raisins, yogurt, and bread crumbs, along with chopped fresh sage and rosemary. Add salt and pepper to taste.

7) Add the above mixture to the hollow in the squash that you made by scooping out the seeds. Return the stuffed squash to the oven for 10-20 minutes.

You can eat the seeds that you set aside, too! Separate the seeds from the stringy flesh that you scooped out, rinse the seeds in a colander, and pat them dry. Then, toss the seeds with olive oil or butter and salt and roast in the oven.

St. Martin of Tours, pray for us!

We Begin Again

The year began waiting for Jesus' first coming; his Advent at Christmas. Then we celebrated the Christ Child and the light He brought. But soon we were forced to contemplate the purpose of his coming; to die as the sacrificial lamb. We fasted through Lent, feasted during Easter, and rejoiced at the coming of the Paraclete at Pentecost. During Ordinary Time, the Scripture readings showed us the growth and persecution of the early Church while also reminding us that Christ is victorious. The scriptures that close the Christian Year reflect this victory in Christ's return; his second Advent when he will come, not in humility, but glory. This recognition that we are, in fact, waiting for Christ's second coming is a perfect way to transition back into the season of Advent.

And, so, we begin again. We participate once again in the life of Christ and the life of the Church. But this rhythm does not become tired or monotonous. Instead, the meaning deepens. We see new significance and come to appreciate things we missed before. The mileposts of the Christian Year begin to stand out, not as meaningless times of distraction, but as important signs pointing us to Christ. So, jump right in! Watch, pray, fast, and, just as importantly, FEAST!

Thank You!

Thank you for supporting us by purchasing our book and sharing the liturgical seasons with us. We'd love to hear from you and see how you're bringing faith into your home. Drop by Carrots for Michaelmas and say hello or tag your Instagrams of your culinary celebrations with #feastbook so we can follow you!

Made in the USA
Middletown, DE
26 September 2017